The Art of Leadership

The Art of Leadership

Abbot Primate Notker Wolf
Sister Enrica Rosanna
with Leo G. Linder

Translated by Gerlinde Büchinger-Schmid
Edited by Sue Bollans

LITURGICAL PRESS
Collegeville, Minnesota

www.litpress.org

Cover design by Ann Blattner. Photo: Thinkstock by Getty Images.

Originally published under the title DIE KUNST, MENSCHEN ZU FÜHREN. Copyright © 2007 Rowohlt Verlag GmbH, Reinbeck bei Hamburg.

All quotations from the Rule of St. Benedict are taken from *The Rule of St. Benedict in English: RB 1980*, ed. Timothy Fry et al. (Collegeville, MN: Liturgical Press, 1981).

1   2   3   4   5   6   7   8   9

Library of Congress Cataloging-in-Publication Data

Wolf, Notker.
    [Kunst, Menschen zu führen. English]
    The art of leadership / by Abbot Primate Notker Wolf, Sister Enrica Rosanna with Leo G. Linder ; translated by Gerlinde Büchinger-Schmid ; edited by Sue Bollans.
        pages   cm
    ISBN 978-0-8146-3810-1 — ISBN 978-0-8146-3835-4 (ebook)
    1. Leadership—Religious aspects—Catholic Church.   2. Benedict, Saint, Abbot of Monte Cassino. Regula.   I. Title.

BV4597.53.L43W6513   2013
253—dc23   2013015828

Contents

CHAPTER 1

The Eternal Good Example

On the Present-Day Relevance of Benedict's Rule

Abbot Primate Notker Wolf

It was no easy task that awaited me when I was elected archabbot of St. Ottilien in 1977. I was now responsible not only for the abbey and its 180 monks but also for our monasteries in Asia and Africa, North and South America, because St. Ottilien is a mission monastery. In addition, I was appointed at a time of radical change. In the German monasteries (as in European monasteries in general), the authority of the abbot was increasingly being challenged. While previously in an undisputed position, the abbots suddenly found themselves on permanent probation. They had to explain, justify, and defend their decisions, and they were finding that their style of leadership was no longer accepted without comment. Outside Europe a new era was also dawning for monasteries because we were changing over to mixed communities in which European and local confrères and sisters lived in the same monastery. This, especially in Africa, did not always go smoothly.

Valuable years of apprenticeship in the art of leadership then lay before me as archabbot. Everywhere, whether in my familiar home monastery or our monasteries outside Europe, we now had to jump over the long shadows of the past, revive the old Benedictine community spirit, and find new, less restricted forms of coexistence and cooperation without eroding the abbot's basic authority. I can count my blessings that in those years I was supported by two great masters. One was our founder, Saint Benedict of Nursia, whose Rule served me from day one as a guide to wise leadership. The other was my then-prior Paulus, to whom I owe countless practical examples of prudent management. Now, as abbot primate with responsibility for the Benedictine Order as a whole, I am still profiting from the experience of these two men. I would therefore like to say first of all what it was I learned from them.

"This eternal [task of being a] good role model is slowly killing me. . . ." This heartfelt complaint came from my old prior and, like much of what he said, was not meant to be taken absolutely seriously, for Prior Paulus did not have to make a huge effort in order to be a model for me and others. He was what he was; he did not to have to pretend. I wish all brothers could be like him, so imperturbable, so unerringly critical, so mercilessly open (when the situation called for it), and so loyal. But Prior Paulus was— fortunately or unfortunately—unique: a giant of a man from an Allgäu farming family, son of the mayor, vested with the invaluable gift of taking none too seriously and observing life from the lofty vantage point of someone who takes himself least seriously of all. I can see him during Divine Office facing me in the choir of my old monastery, St. Ottilien: one moment immersed in a psalm text and the next with a quite perceptible grin crossing his face—probably because he had just thought of someone who had been high-handed with him and had been taken down a peg or two in the manner for which he was famous.

Not all the qualities that distinguished him when he was a prior were innate. He started working on himself at a young age, and when he was only a student he developed an almost sporting ambition to become so self-possessed that nothing and no one would irritate him. This decision originated from an experience in the mid-1920s in the St. Ottilien seminary for missions, where one of his instructors was a priest who was constantly running down the monastery and his confrères in front of the students. He and two of his friends swore at the time that they would never allow themselves to make the same mistake; they put a piggybank in their dormitory and undertook to pay ten cents for every uncontrolled outburst of anger or indignation. Later Prior Paulus told me, "After half a year we had ourselves under control. Since then no one has been able to get us worked up." Each of the three subsequently joined a monastery, and each maintained an impressive inner freedom throughout his life.

When I had long been archabbot of St. Ottilien my prior visited one of our monasteries in Africa, and over breakfast with the German sisters he related the story of this victory over lack of self-control. That was something they had learned a long time ago, said the sisters. Nothing could ruffle them anymore, nothing could annoy them. One of these sisters had kindly cleaned his shoes because he was now old and stiff. Minutes later my prior removed a shoe with a groan, examined it from all sides, poked around in the sole with a knife, and straightened up. "Look, sister," he said with an angelic expression on his face, "there is still a bit of dirt under here. . . ." "You should have seen the sisters: they all simultaneously hit the roof!" he said when he told me about it. And my old prior? He just grinned.

Not everyone got along with Prior Paulus, and not all of the four abbots under whom my old prior served at the monastery over a period of nearly forty years knew how to take him. Nothing fazed him, but his steadfastness unsettled other people and some found his straightforwardness threatening. One of my predecessors at St. Ottilien even dismissed him as prior, but he had to reinstate him because it caused an uproar in the community. It was only in the face of death that the two were really able to talk. The abbot, who was suffering from terminal cancer, sent for him and finally confessed, "Father Prior, now at last I believe that you were not after my job." No, it was certainly not always easy to be an abbot under Prior Paul.

He never had any ambitions to be an abbot himself. When another monastery wanted to elect him abbot he declined briefly, saying: "I will never wear a mitre on my head." Did he shrink from responsibility? That was hardly the case. As a prior he was the ideal person, the perfect second man. But he shunned the limelight and the concessions to religious masquerade that the office of abbot would have demanded of him. As the second in rank he felt freer. As an abbot he would have had to bow more to hierarchical pomp than was compatible with his disdain for subservience to authority and to status symbols. His aversion to every display of power sometimes even expressed itself in sarcasm, and I must confess that over time I came to adopt his attitude. I was guided very much by some of his comments, and every time I enter the Vatican his words come to mind: "Do you know, Father Abbot, what was the darkest day in the history of mankind? The day when the bishops adorned themselves for the first time with the insignia" (the emblems such as the mitre, cross, and crozier). Then this giant of a man took a breath and continued in a louder voice, "But much, much darker was the day when the abbots imitated the bishops!"

The "eternal good example" of my prior had a highly instructive effect on me, at any rate. What did I learn from him? That you can go a long way with humor and self-irony, whether you are responsible as an abbot for 180 monks or as abbot primate for 25,000 monks and nuns. That by being straightforward you can go even further. And that you can go unexpectedly far if you are impressed neither by crimson cardinal robes nor the titles of presidents, nor by company cars and reserved parking places next to the garage exit. In other words, Prior Paul showed me what authority could and should be. He opened my eyes to the benefit authority can bring when the shell of authority is discarded so as to reveal what it really involves: responsibility, care, service. Released from its trappings, authority can develop its liberating, mind- and soul-freeing power.

In this respect above all, Prior Paul was an exemplary Christian, because what he did is in accordance with the teachings of Jesus Christ and is what Christianity should constantly do: challenge all false values, destroy all false glory, and expose all arrogated authority as vain and empty. In addition, Prior Paul was a leader in the spirit of our founder, St. Benedict of Nursia. When you study the Rule Benedict gave to his monasteries as a kind of constitution for the journey through the centuries, the notion of authority as embodied by my prior occurs repeatedly, with the only difference being that Benedict always expressed it in rather more serious terms than those employed by Prior Paul.

Benedict considered authority only justifiable and good when official power was paired with concern for each individual, when it was combined with respect for individuality, different abilities, and particular personal needs. When Benedict thus endows the abbot with far-reaching powers, this is not only because someone has to have the final say but because he understands authority as an instance that helps, supports, encourages, and exhorts, and is constantly mindful of the progress and welfare of those who are subject to it. The purpose of real authority is therefore always to help people to become more independent and discover what lies within their capabilities: in other words, help them to become free.

This is how I understand Benedict. This is why I find his Rule humane and wise. But is it also still relevant? It was written fifteen hundred years ago, when societies were disintegrating as the ancient world came to an end with the decline of the Western Roman Empire. Can important ideas about the art of leadership still be derived from it today? Let us take a closer look at Benedict's Rule. It actually regulates surprisingly little, concentrating primarily on practical matters such as the daily routine of the community, dealing with the property of the monastery, the Psalm sequence of the Divine Office. Benedict's reflections repeatedly revolve around the following questions: what qualifies someone to lead others? How should one approach the task, how much consideration should he or she have and how much forbearance, how strict should he or she be? And how can the abbot use authority in such a way as to create an atmosphere in the monastery that gives people space to develop? In a word, in his Rule, Benedict's main concern is to formulate the essential qualities of the leader and set standards for a leadership that is both efficient and humane. These standards are, I believe, therefore also timelessly valid, because they are rooted in the biblical image of humanity, in Christian anthropology.

In my opinion there is no image of humanity more realistic than this, no description of the *conditio humana* that is more apt. Why? Because Christian anthropology reflects the fundamental contradictions of the human being, who is first the creature and image of God and is hence equipped with worth, with human dignity, and is therefore inviolable, in fact, holy—and who is, second, also weak, fallible and corruptible, in other words, a sinner. This view of humanity has practical implications for dealing with people, because the Christian faith provides me with an ideal foundation for mutual respect and at the same time constantly motivates me to show this respect again and again. It is no longer at my discretion to respect human dignity in one case and disregard it in another. Respect has become an immutably valid principle of my conduct, also with regard to the more disagreeable representatives of the human race. The border official who dealt with me on my last visit to North Korea, for example, was not very nice. He was not even polite. I would have had every reason to be angry over the way he treated me, but I was not, because the thought first passed through my head that this man was created by God and is just as much loved by God as God loves you.

At the same time we must be aware that we are never dealing with angels of light. People are more or less strong or weak, and we are all subject to envy, dislike, willfulness, and even deceit. This awareness preserves us from disappointment. It makes us compassionate and also alert to the uniqueness of people and situations. So there is no room for credulity, naïveté, do-gooderism, but instead we must meet the challenge of taking human shortcomings into account without also passing judgment on them.

This Christian realism runs throughout the Rule on which the lives of our monastics have been oriented from the beginning of our existence as an Order. Consequently, the Rule does not subject the community to rigid laws for combating evil; instead, it shows it the way according to certain principles. The abbot has the role of one who applies the Rule to the concrete case, the concrete human being, and on occasion modifies it or accommodates it as necessary. Benedict did not attempt to bring people into line by means of painfully precise directives. He knew all too well that every person is unique, but none is perfect, and that therefore any stringent method or thoroughly rationalistic technique for leading people must fail. Benedict did not have a "program." Therefore he accorded all the more significance to the personal qualities of those who exercise the leadership functions. They cannot retreat behind the Rule when things get critical; they cannot hide behind its prescriptions. Rather, they must constantly allow their suitability for office to be questioned, constantly remember their responsibility, constantly permit themselves to be measured by the standards Benedict proposed. And they must do all that with the goal of finding the correct measure in thought, speech, and action. For that is what is at stake above all: being modest leaders who act reasonably, have a sense of proportion, and measure up to their own standards. Only in that way can they find harmony between the Rule and the realities of life.

In other words, Benedict's Rule bears the hallmarks of a person who is convinced of the meaning of freedom and the value of the individual. This guarantees the Rule's durability—and I am not alone in thinking this. In fireside chats or presentations I am repeatedly amused to see how amazed politicians and representatives of the business world are when a quotation from Benedict's Rule fits the actual current problem or the present situation as if it had been written with these in mind. Moreover, we Benedictines could not look back on a successful history of nearly fifteen hundred years' duration if this Rule had not proven itself under all circumstances and conditions. A Benedictine monastery is virtually indestructible, except by external violence. And today it is evident that not even globalization can affect the validity of this Rule; in our Asian, African, and American monasteries there is daily evidence that it is compatible with the identity of the widest variety of cultures.

Benedict has thus been a considerable source of inspiration for this book, in which I am concerned as little with the brilliant boss, the perfect teacher, or the model parents as Benedict was with making his monastery an elite training center for the ideal Christian. Nobody is perfect. That, of course, includes me. Delegating, for example. . . . Delegating really isn't my forte. I can just about allow my secretary, Father Henry, to organize the next Congress of Abbots, but I do all the correspondence myself. Perhaps this is why

I never finish my work. (I help myself by doing everything right away, immediately—and the rest at some point.) No, we must not drive the devil of human imperfection out with the Beelzebub of perfectionism. You can, incidentally, live quite well with a lot of weaknesses, and not even the vanity my old prior loved to mock necessarily prevents you from being a good leader. I once knew a CEO who never let anyone forget his imaginary laurel wreath. He was always making incidental remarks to show what the company and humankind owed him. His achievements certainly did merit recognition, and the man himself was very likeable—and in fact his successor's modesty did not make the latter any more human.

Nevertheless, knowledge and expertise alone qualify no one for a position of leadership. Whenever a company issue involves people, management must become leadership. People cannot be managed. The moment superiors treat cases that call for leadership in the same way as financial or production matters, they start acting on a purely theoretical basis, and even the best mathematician can be a torture for his students as a teacher. Of course, I know that people are hired not to take it easy but to contribute to the work and the profits. However, in my opinion you cannot separate the person from the job. Work must be human. Purely profit-oriented management destroys the working atmosphere, undermines the motivation of employees, and reduces their efficiency. In contrast, real humanity pays off in the long run; a people-friendly corporate culture must therefore be in the interest of any company's management. This nevertheless raises the question: can the art of leadership be learned?

I think not. At any rate, leadership qualities cannot be acquired systematically in coaching seminars like other forms of knowledge, nor can personality deficiencies be concealed by means of well-rehearsed gestures. There are no methods or tricks that can turn a bad leader into a good one, and any subordinate will soon see through a boss who, after attending a leadership seminar, is suddenly able to look as if he or she is listening with concentration. Of course, the mastery of certain techniques can be advantageous, for example, in the area of time management or discussion strategies.

But this is of little use if certain character traits such as sincerity and perseverance are not already inherent, and certain mental abilities like patience have not been acquired with time and experience. However, it is also true that each of us can abuse our charisma and direct our authority against our own team or students; hence, everyone must be very clear about the goals she or he is pursuing as a leader. It will do people with leadership qualities no harm to open their eyes to what is important and render them the same service that my old prior rendered us in his day. This is how Sister Rosanna and I see the task we have undertaken with this book, in which we focus more on the business and political world in the first part and more on schools and education in the second part. We wanted in this way to create a book with two voices, two perspectives, a book in which my experience as a Benedictine monk and the experience of Sister Rosanna as a Salesian Sister and vice-secretary of the Vatican Congregation for Religious complement one another.

Incidentally, as archabbot of St. Ottilien I also had to learn to gradually distance myself from Prior Paul. We continued to like each other, but even he had his limits, and with increasing age he was more and more resistant to change. "Father Archabbot," he said, "don't keep shifting things around, it'll give you trouble in the monastery," and my answer was, "Father Prior, if we don't change anything now, that's when we'll have trouble." However, when you think about it, such experiences also spoke in his favor, simply because I was able to separate myself from him as a person without this detracting in the slightest from his service as an "eternal good role model." And perhaps my old prior has thus provided the most convincing example of true authority.

CHAPTER 2

The Temptations of Power

Personality Is Everything

Abbot Primate Notker Wolf

> In large companies there may be five or six people who have particular authority over you. These people can deprive you of every spark of creativity and vitality. We have bosses who have no vision, rather bland people who are not at all passionate about their work and are only interested in demonstrating that they are somebodies, even though in their profession they're actually nobodies. These people have only their careers in mind and want to earn as much money as possible and be able to feel as important as possible. They love to show other people that they are completely and utterly at their mercy; their standard approach is "Don't think you're special." And they do in fact succeed in making good people look small or at least in making them seriously doubt their own abilities.

This complaint about unsuitable managers was made to me by an editor at a German broadcasting corporation. It is perhaps not typical, but it describes typical mistakes made by managers when dealing with coworkers and subordinates, and it puts the consequences in a nutshell. These need no explanation; everyone has experienced the effect bad leadership can have on work satisfaction (and results); you only need to have had an inadequate teacher at school. But the causes of poor leadership ought to be investigated.

The great, ever-present danger is that of succumbing to the temptation of power. No one is entirely immune to this. The despotic form of power is usually valued by those whose own achievements are insignificant, people who feel small, unbearably small, and exert their power to compensate for their own shortcomings. Their delusions of grandeur are rooted in an inferiority complex, or let's say in the unsettling knowledge that they are not as strong as someone in their position should be. The best example is the cold-blooded climber, the traditional careerist who has never had the necessary competence but has always had the best connections, who swore at the age of twenty-five: "At forty, I'll be at the top"—and at forty really is at the top.

What does power mean to such people? I suspect that it is in any case a huge relief, because their position in the hierarchy frees them from the constant fear of being ignored. And that's their problem. The ruthless, over-ambitious person is in fact merely the extreme example of a type I have also occasionally encountered in my sphere. Not at peace with themselves, such people suffer from an almost pathological need for appreciation. They are in a state of total anxiety about themselves. If you pat such a person on the right shoulder, she will offer you the left as well. His insatiable hunger for respect goes so far that he only rises in his own estimation when he can say he once sat next to this or that well-known personality, with whom he perhaps even exchanged a few words. I frequently find that someone only wants to talk to me so that she can bask in my "glory" and subsequently have a better opinion of herself! If such people move up the ladder, power offers them a welcome escape from their dependence on the applause of others. Suddenly they find it quite tolerable to be disliked. They in fact enjoy not having to worry about their popularity. And they demonstrate their power by making as many people as possible feel "I am not the slightest bit interested in being acknowledged by you. And the fact that you despise me doesn't bother me either."

Is there any advice these people can be given? None at all, I fear. For their own purposes it is enough to split the staff neatly into friends and enemies and play the enemies off against each other, using every trick in the book—and even their friends are probably regarded simply as useful idiots. They will always thrust themselves into the limelight, employ tactical maneuvers, and serve their vanity more than the common cause. Presumably such power-obsessed people only come to their senses when the thing they fear most actually happens: they lose their power. Their self-confidence, their entire identity, depends on their power position, and only when they lose their battles might it dawn on them how empty is the happiness they pursue and how empty they themselves are. Or else they rebel and become brutal.

Of course, we must distinguish between career and careerism. Careerism means trampling on others in order to be promoted, or knuckling under for the same reason and keeping your head down. However, pursuing a career is in itself neither good nor bad, and there is no doubt that the person who wants to achieve and share responsibility for something and is eager for new, attractive tasks must and will be promoted. It's also liberating and satisfying to finally overcome restrictions and obstacles that have prevented us from developing. We should not forget that our own self-esteem is at stake when promotion is a long time coming. Inevitably we wonder what we did wrong, whether we are inept or are standing in someone's way. Few people reject an offer that confirms their abilities and moves them up the career ladder, and I have not infrequently encountered monks who desperately wanted to become abbots. This is human, although it is not necessarily a Benedictine attribute. Moreover, we should have no illusions about the driving force of ambition and vanity. There is no doubt that both are a powerful motivation for exceptional achievement.

However, it is not only the weaker natures who succumb to the temptations of power. Really good people are also in considerable danger of losing their grip on reality. You can get used to being courted, and it's a glorious feeling to be idolized. You puff up with pride, your imaginary laurel wreath takes shape, and slowly but surely the belief ripens in you that everything is your doing. Every success is credited to your own account. From then on you regard self-indulgence and vanity as justifiable pride, and finally you are no longer in any doubt that you can do everything better than other people and know better than everyone else. In addition, self-importance will be imposed on you by bootlickers and claques who constantly whisper in your ear that no one is more competent than you. It's a fact that people in leadership positions who are doing a good job cannot defend themselves against being praised to the skies. Maybe they don't want to. I am reminded of the sessions of a previous German State Cabinet, which invariably began with tributes to the Minister President, a proper act of adoration—and this is certainly not an isolated case.

Once self-importance has insinuated itself, it can have disastrous effects. One is the loss of a sense of reality. If everyone thinks you are special, there is no reason for you not to think you are special too and start seeing any criticism as fundamentally inappropriate or the work of a malicious maverick. At some point unvarnished assessments of the situation also fall into the category of unmerited criticism, and self-important individuals gradually lose contact with reality. They are no longer aware of what is going on, because self-importance is isolating and isolated people are easily prey to suspicion. Since they now only hear what they want to hear, they rely on spies and informers to find out what is said about them and how much of what they hear is not meant sincerely. In this way they destroy the last vestiges of their staff's trust and become even more isolated. Here I think of those incredible, forceful, old-style German CEOs, whom no one dares tell the truth for fear of being rebuked and relegated. They are guided solely by their own brilliant inspirations, quite often with the result that they throw millions or even billions out of the window because they are blind to reality.

In the past the court jester may have helped in such cases. Now that those have gone out of fashion, high-ranking people are expected to cope with censure and frankness regardless of where it comes from so that no one who dares to criticize makes a fool of herself. Here I am reminded of a passage from our Rule. In Chapter 61 Benedict talks about hospitality and the accommodation of visiting monks in the monastery. First he says that if a person who has come from afar does not make unreasonable demands, he may stay as long as he desires. And then he continues: "He may, indeed, with all humility and love make some reasonable criticisms or observations, which the abbot should prudently consider; it is possible that the Lord guided him to the monastery for this very purpose." This is wise. Benedict knows how easy it is to become professionally blinkered. Therefore he says: Think twice, my dear abbot, whether the man might not be right. It may be embarrassing, this criticism from an outsider, but do not be so foolish as to assiduously ignore it. This sentence from the Rule of Saint Benedict should in my opinion be hung on the wall of every boardroom.

The person who betrays the trust of her employees through her own self-importance is in any case no good as a leader, simply because productive cooperation with her is impossible. But there are other manifestations of the power trip. One is the greed that tempts top executives to give each other astronomical salaries and huge golden handshakes. I would never be stingy with managers; they should be well paid. But their salaries already include a sizeable risk premium, so what is the justification for severance packages approaching a million dollars? In fact, they walk away with compensation twice, three times, and four times that amount. When they can shamelessly pocket such sums they are lacking all sense of proportion, wanting in exactly what Benedict considers to be the essential virtue of a leader: moderation. It is possible that such managers still do a good job, but they are not suitable leaders because they are failing miserably in their task of setting an example and are thus acting irresponsibly.

Finally, power is ultimately tempting because of the pronounced status consciousness of many managers, expressed in the status symbols with which we are all too familiar, or reflected by all the things top executives do to surround themselves with an aura of grandeur or the way they emphasize their authority by distancing themselves very visibly from their subordinates. Let me put it quite frankly: status symbols merely serve the purpose of flattering their owners. They are nothing but a framework to which people cling when deep down they are afraid of losing their authority.

The Orthodox exarch who studied with us some years ago was a particularly bizarre example of status consciousness. He was recognizable by his tall headgear and dignified gait. At the very beginning he had bad results in an exam, and he was horrified. According to him, as an Orthodox dignitary he was entitled to better marks. He had internalized the authority of his office to such an extent that as a student he claimed the same deference he expected as an official. He therefore took a brilliant assessment for granted as commensurate with his status. I always think of this exarch when I occasionally hear of the wrangling for company cars, office space, corner offices, and secretaries. "Where status symbols are concerned," someone who knows what he's talking about once said to me, "in a company, kindergarten goes on to the age of sixty-five"—words that might have been spoken by my old prior.

It is not that I consider symbols essentially superfluous. Communication with large masses of people, for example, is only possible by means of symbolic gestures. Pope Benedict XVI demonstrated this on his trip to Turkey, when he took the Turkish flag and waved it in front of everyone—a symbolic gesture that had public appeal. I also find symbols that warn against the temptations of power appropriate, like those three burning haystacks on St. Peter's Square, which a newly elected pope used to have to pass on the way to his coronation in St. Peter's Basilica. These were symbols of mortality with an unmistakable message: keep your feet on the ground, don't let yourself be blinded by all the pomp, don't forget that you share the same fate as the rest of humankind and will one day turn to dust and ashes. However, on no account should symbols represent power in the old lordly manner and widen the gap between superiors and subordinates. Here we see the great mistake made by all those who have succumbed to the temptation of power: they feel more confident of their authority the greater they distance themselves from others, whereas they should be doing the opposite: seeking to get closer to others and keeping a distance from themselves, because that is the secret of true authority.

This may come as a surprise. But I am convinced that a person who cannot get away from himself, who yearns for recognition and success—as described above—cannot see things in their proper perspective, and that distorted vision makes him blind to the requirements of the task at hand and inevitably leads him to misjudge people and situations. The authority and influence of a leader therefore largely depend on how free he is of himself. This means he must not worry about his halo. His own person must not play any further role. He must learn to keep a distance from himself. Only someone who gets the better of himself will acquire internal autonomy, and only then will he be able to assess people and circumstances properly, use his authority purposefully, summon the necessary patience and, when necessary, also show considerable perseverance. You can only develop your leadership skills if you are prepared to restrain your own self as far as possible: in other words, if you experience inner freedom.

There is nothing new about this. Even the Bible shows how the person seeking herself destroys herself, because the more she concentrates on her own person, the emptier and poorer she emerges from this search. It is for this reason that St. Benedict assigns particular value to humility in his Rule, in the sense not of subservience but of distance to oneself. It is one of the wonderful paradoxes of life that this humility makes a person not weaker but stronger, because she is then liberated from hubris, from obsession with power, and from pressure to succeed. Jesus sums up this paradox in two sentences when he says: "Whoever wishes to save his life will lose it, but whoever loses his life for my sake will find it." What this means for us is that, if we want to exercise true authority and not arbitrary power, we must stop worrying about our own importance.

What this inner freedom does, if anything, is to make us resistant to the drug of power. And it is now, under these conditions, that we can use our authority responsibly, namely, for the benefit of those we lead. The crucial question with regard to the art of leadership is therefore: how do I understand my authority? Do I use it to uplift or to devalue people? Do I recognize that someone is doing a good job and do all I can to encourage him? Or do I think about how I can take him down a peg or two at the earliest opportunity? This is what determines not only the work climate but also the success of any manager, because in the long run no worker, no employee, will passively accept a form of dependency that makes him feel incapacitated, but anyone will willingly enter into a relationship of dependency that offers opportunities for development one would not otherwise have had. True authority ultimately generates a feeling of mutual responsibility and creates the best conditions for fruitful cooperation at all levels.

To round off this chapter I would just like to point out that in the time of St. Benedict the situation was apparently not much different from what it is today. He must also have had difficulties with the self-importance of certain people. In any case, Benedict is nowhere more outspoken and adamant than in the chapter of his Rule that deals with the acceptance of priests into the community of his monastery. Ironically, it is the priests whom he perceives as thinking themselves better than other people. It is they alone he suspects primarily of arrogance and vanity. I have to smile every time I read in Chapter 62 of his Rule how he targeted the priests of his day. He warns that if a priest asks for admission into the monastery it should not be agreed to immediately. If such a priest nevertheless persists in his request, he must be made to understand that he will "have to observe the full discipline of the Rule without any mitigation." And then, a few paragraphs further on, Benedict is even more explicit: the priest should "not presume to do anything except what the abbot commands him. . . . Just because he is a priest, he may not therefore forget the obedience and discipline of the Rule. . . . should he presume to act otherwise, he must be regarded as a rebel, not as a priest. . . ." You don't even have to read between the lines to understand that humility cannot have been the strong point of the priests in those days and that the arrogance of individuals was perceived even in the sixth century as a threat to what we would today call team spirit.

CHAPTER 3

You Have to Like People

The Company as an Anxiety-Free Space

Abbot Primate Notker Wolf

He was a wily strategist, the department head of a large European authority who was described to me by one of his employees. Cool, calculating and—dreaded. "He knew exactly how to make us feel insecure. His strategy was unpredictability, his disciplinary measures calculated changes of mood," she said.

> If the day before yesterday you were in his favor, the next day you weren't, only to be taken up graciously again twenty-four hours later. With a frosty smile he could give you the feeling you had done everything wrong, just to remind you whose favor you depended on. Intimidating you and then taking you into his confidence, behaving in a fatherly way, and then acting like a tyrant and a raging demigod again—it was a constant rollercoaster of emotions. Many people suffered under him, but it was clear to everyone that they all replaceable and no one could expect loyalty in case of doubt. And with this ploy he actually had everyone under his thumb.

Yes, this is one way of managing a department, by knowing how to make your subordinates submissive and yourself as boss unassailable. But you can't manage human beings that way. You can't lead people in such a way because people need freedom, especially when they are supposed to be producing good work, which is why wherever efficiency and performance are what counts, employees have to be free people. And that is why one of the most important tasks of humane leadership is to prevent sycophancy.

There is no need for the subtle terror of leaders who behave arbitrarily and operate with psychological tricks. In every company there is a risk of everyone just saying yes and amen to whatever comes from the top. But the success of a company ultimately depends on the self-assurance of its employees. And this places responsibility on every manager, whose task is to promote and maintain the self-confidence of subordinates. Frightened staff are of no value to a company because they are not creative—they automatically go on the defensive and instead of contributing to the creative process, they become inhibited. Therefore the first principle of wise leadership is not to be a brilliant boss but to be able to create an atmosphere in which no one becomes a sycophant. What is needed is humane working atmosphere, an anxiety-free space in which all the employees are able to apply their skills without fear of embarrassing themselves or being lambasted. How can this be done?

First of all, as I see it, you must be ready to acknowledge the existence of the employees. This already requires a good measure of self-discipline: if you often see others only out of the corner of your eye because you are so full of yourself, you sort them by position and importance and rush past those of lesser significance. You must discipline yourself daily, hourly, to see them properly. And then of course you must greet them, but not in passing, not out of duty, so that they say aha, the boss has ticked me off her list for today. Use too many words rather than too few. How grateful people are became clear to me again when I exchanged a few words with the waiting camera team during a papal visit and one of them said to me, "You are one of the very few people who realizes that we exist."

So never give anyone the feeling they are being essentially ignored. In the monastery I certainly take the time to speak to anyone who is "down" and ask, "What's the matter?" Many people are pleased to be able to talk. I know that in a company where everyone goes home at the end of the working day it is not possible to have as much time for one another, but even there a lot can be achieved by kindness expressed without any ulterior motive, and often a glance, a pat on the shoulder, is enough. It is only important to remember that in the interpersonal area we should never deliberately try to create a particular effect, because as soon as someone feels that kindness is being shown just to keep him happy, he will lower the shutters. We are all allergic to crude attempts to condition us. In other words, the bottom line is that you have to like people, genuinely like them, if a relaxed, humane working atmosphere is to be achieved. There is a wonderful word for this: benevolence.

By that I do not mean naïve good humor but a wholehearted curiosity about other people. Out of benevolence I take a closer look at the person I am dealing with and find out more and more about her. Without benevolence my intuition is not the slightest bit useful, because I will judge people through the lens of my suspicion and will only be concerned about not missing any alarm signals. But benevolence will open my eyes to the whole person, to everything that is remarkable about her, to everything that is worth encouraging and may not be obvious. It enables me to obtain a realistic understanding of what drives and motivates her and identify characteristics she might never have noticed in herself. It also prevents me from making assumptions and misjudging and unintentionally humiliating people.

Benevolence of this kind has nothing to do with softness. One can be unfailingly friendly but at the same time unyielding. In difficult situations in particular you will discover that this tranquil, imperturbable friendliness can be spectacularly effective.

During the general chapter convened for the election of an abbot in East Asia, a young monk suddenly got up, looked at me, and asked caustically, "What are you actually doing here today, you Europeans?" An icy wind swept through the hall at that moment. People lowered their heads; no one said anything. And I thought, should I throw the culprit out? Or at least rebuke him sharply? As archabbot I would have had the right to do so. I hesitated. At that moment my gaze fell on a German confrère who had been living in that particular country for a long time, and I remembered an incident from our time as students together. I had got thoroughly worked up over some piece of unpleasantness, and this very con-frère followed me to my room to say, "Notker, today you really disappointed me. I always admired you so much, because you never got ruffled. And now. . . ." It was a valuable memory. And I did succeed in not seeming unfriendly when I said to this young monk, "You know, I'm doing my duty here according to the stat-utes, and then I'm going home." That was all. But the situation was defused. The election took place without further disturbance. And afterward the elder confrères came to me, kissed my hands, and apologized for the rudeness of their colleague. Had I thrown him out, the situation would probably have ended differently. Then I might also have antagonized the old confrères. In this way I had won them over—and maybe that young hothead of a monk as well.

And what if kindness is too much to expect or would be inappro-priate? I long ago made it a rule for myself that everyone, absolutely everyone, is at least entitled to an objective response. At all meet-ings—whether in the past in my home monastery of St. Ottilien, or now in Sant' Anselmo—I have always tried to respond to everyone as objectively as possible. If a remark or a question had nothing to do with what we were talking about, I tried patiently to explain the reason why; if someone raised an objection that had already been dealt with, I calmly explained the matter once more—so that I was sometimes rebuked afterwards because I did not tell the person off on behalf of the others at the meeting. But I always said to myself, "Don't reprimand anybody. It's better to react calmly to the silliest objection than to have people with intelligent objections afraid to open their mouths." Creating an anxiety-free space actually requires the person in charge to have a lot of patience and great self-control at times. You have to discipline yourself even when your pulse is racing, your heart is thumping, and you are about to explode. This is the price for an atmosphere in which every employee can be sure of having his ideas listened to. It is a pleasure to work in such an atmosphere; it is positively exhilarating. We have all had this experience. With me at least, even the shyest and craziest should not be afraid to speak out—which is why those who only want to provoke or make pomp-ous pronouncements also get a strictly objective response from me.

Let us go a step further. Let us not be content to interact with our employees with friendly attentiveness and patience. Let us try also to be fair to everyone by taking the uniqueness, the very personal nature and special abilities as well as the characteristic weaknesses of every individual, into account. Benedict saw this respect for the uniqueness of the individual as a major challenge for any leader. The abbot, he writes in the second chapter of his Rule, "must know what a difficult and demanding burden he has undertaken: directing souls and serving a variety of temperaments coaxing, reproving, and encouraging them as appropriate. He must . . . accommodate and adapt himself to each one's character and intelligence. . . ." This demands a great deal of an abbot. It is, as Benedict says, an arduous task. Hence in his Rule he repeatedly goes into detail about this, encouraging the monks to express their personal wishes to the cellarer, the administrator of the monastery, and even conceding them the right to object if an order is too much for them. It repeatedly amazes me how much value this sixth-century man accords to the individual. Everyone is to be treated as an individual case. And to do this the abbot must know his people well.

What applies to the abbot, in my opinion, applies to managers in general. Sensitivity and an understanding of human nature are indispensable prerequisites not only for a humane working climate but also for the success of a company in general. A boss must be able to perceive the shortcomings and development potential of her subordinates and judge whether they are reliable. But more is expected of her than knowing the strengths and weaknesses of her employees. She is the one who must know how to deal with all the hopes, aspirations, and resentments, and with all the hidden and open ambitions of her people. She must not wound their pride, undermine them, or call them into question as persons. Employees must believe in themselves, whether they have made one mistake or five. The manager must not trigger defense mechanisms and should therefore be aware of every individual's Achilles heel. One of the biggest problems is repeatedly having to deal with people who are very quick to take offense, who sense hostility at every turn and leap gratefully into the path of the arrow just in order to be struck and be able to shoot back. Such people may be the opposite of sycophants, but they are just as unlikely to turn out to be constructive members of a company's workforce. People in leadership positions thus need an incredible sense of what makes the other person tick to avoid triggering any defense mechanisms.

I shall return to this topic later when I talk about handling conflicts, but here I would like to give another reason why the ability to put oneself in someone else's place is constantly in demand even in everyday situations. It often happens that we react with irritation to the slow-wittedness of an employee and immediately doubt his intelligence. And it may well be that this person is not necessarily one of the brightest. But often we also simply forget how much more familiar we are with a particular task than the other person. What appears obvious to us because it occupies us constantly or because our frame of reference is quite different may be unfamiliar territory for him or extend beyond the limits of his imagination. Here again, patience is called for. Let us therefore not be too quick to conclude that the other person lacks the necessary brainpower. Let us rather initially assume that he is simply out of his depth due to lack of information, and let us take the time to instruct him.

By being sensitive to employees, taking them seriously, and treating them as individuals, you have already gone a long way toward creating a humane working climate. In my experience one more thing is necessary: a sincere attempt to create trust. I am convinced that fruitful cooperation is never possible without mutual trust. Of course, a person who is only interested in exploiting her power, who pushes subordinates about like pieces on a chessboard, can do without trust and can also be untroubled by inefficiency in individual cases so long as no shadow falls on him. But authority depends on trust. The authority of a manager is based on the trust placed in her and her willingness to trust others.

Where there is trust, a solid, humane, and legal basis exists, an atmosphere in which all those involved can be sure no one is playing with marked cards or resorting to tricks, base tactics, or dissimulation. It only takes one person who can provide such assurance for the working atmosphere of a whole department to be decidedly improved. And this person need not even fear that his sincerity will sink him. In my experience, in any case, I have had the best results from being open with people and always putting all my cards on the table. Of course, you never know whom you are dealing with at the beginning, but this has never troubled me. I have rarely been disappointed. Rather, I have been able to achieve an unbelievable amount with trust. Had I been more cautious, had I frequently been suspicious, it would not have been so easy for me to mobilize people, overcome resistance, and win hearts, and I would never have discovered how few people consciously abuse the trust placed in them. It seems to me, therefore, that whoever sows trust will in most cases also reap trust, but one who sows mistrust will inevitably reap nothing but mistrust.

However, what you must never do if you want to win trust is fear for your prestige and thus act as if you are infallible. There is virtually nothing that makes people trust you more quickly, or does more to strengthen your own position, than showing awareness of your own shortcomings and admitting faults. Very early in my tenure as the newly appointed archabbot of St. Ottilien, I was required in my very first few days to hold a chapter meeting, but I was not quite familiar with the practice, and I was also known to many brothers only by name because I had spent the previous years in Rome. Shortly before the meeting my cellarer came to me and said that there was a financial matter that was not on the agenda. We'll include it, I decided, and get it over with in one go. The matter went through. But as I left the chapter hall after the meeting I suddenly realized that I had just made a formal mistake. Such matters must first be discussed in the Senior Council, a small advisory committee that marshals the arguments in advance and takes an initial vote so that discussions in the chapter are not too time consuming. And straight away my old prior had come up to me to say, "Most Reverend Father, I believe we have done something stupid today."

I realized that this faux pas was by no means harmless. It is particularly annoying for the confrères to be given the impression that somebody is trying to take them by surprise in order to impose his own will. I took the first opportunity to clarify the matter and said at supper, "Dear confrères, we must discuss the financial issue a second time, because the matter first has to be dealt with by the Senior Council. I overlooked that today. Please don't be cross with me, I'm only a beginner." And the result? Resounding laughter—and a voice in the background: "At last we have a Superior who can admit his mistakes." This broke the ice. Now I had won the trust of those who barely knew me, not by an outstanding achievement but by the simple confession of an error. Everyone now knew that the new abbot was not out to deceive them. And they had also understood that under me they too could make mistakes. At any rate, they did not need to be afraid of doing so anymore. The foundation for an anxiety-free space was laid.

It should be clear by now how much depends on the personality of a leader when it is comes to creating an atmosphere of freedom and trust. The less a person reeks of ambition, the easier it will be for him to win the trust of others. The sooner you succeed in keeping yourself prudently in the background, the freer the employees will feel. The better you control your defense reflexes, the more understanding you will have for others. As long as your own personality is like a house of cards, all your energy will be channeled into self-defense and be wasted. If you want to help others, you must know one person particularly well: yourself. For this reason we Benedictines run an annual training course for our own leaders. This repeatedly and primarily focuses on self-reflection, because one's attitude toward oneself is crucial for good leadership. How much does applause mean to me? How really unbiased am I? Am I mature enough to face facts and call a spade a spade? Sooner or later you inevitably encounter a basic problem of leadership: the tension between your own drives and the demands of your task.

It is a fact that a person who builds a career owes her success in large part to her ambition, assertiveness, and perhaps not least her desire to be in the limelight, or at least one of the characters at center stage, and thus, to a not inconsiderable degree, to egocentrism. On the other hand, as a manager she is often expected to make herself as invisible as possible and to show great restraint, sometimes even to the point of self-denial. This leads to tension between one's personality and one's job, tension that must be endured. It can bring one to the breaking point or, ideally, it can create a person who achieves a balance between unobtrusiveness and forceful action, who knows what she wants but patronizes no one, who is aware of her responsibility and still gives others the impression that they, not she, are the center of things. This is someone who behaves entirely in the spirit of the Chinese philosopher Lao Tzu, who says:

> The best rulers are those whom the people hardly know exist.
> Next come rulers whom the people love and praise.
> After that come rulers whom the people fear.
> And the worst rulers are those whom the people despise.
> The ruler who does not trust the people will not be trusted
>   by the people.
> The best ruler stays in the background, and his voice is rarely
>   heard.
> When he accomplishes his tasks, and things go well,
> The people declare: it was we who did it by ourselves.

CHAPTER 4

Those Who Can, May

Cooperative Leadership

Abbot Primate Notker Wolf

At the beginning of my tenure as archabbot of St. Ottilien in the late seventies, I had suggested some changes in the monastery and introduced some innovations. I remember saying at the time to a younger confrère, "Good heavens, must all the bright ideas come from me?" whereupon he gave me a sidelong glance and said, "You know what our Benedictine structure is like: The abbot commands and we do what he says. Everything comes from the top." "As of today, it no longer will," I told him. "Remember that."

But I had to agree with him. For centuries our abbots actually felt like rulers who could rely on the blind obedience of their monks. Inside the convent walls they had behaved like autocrats, and even in the early sixties many of our abbeys were still considered places of strict, rigid monastic discipline. There was hardly anything left of the spirit of generous, wise humanitarianism that had inspired Benedict when he drew up his Rule fifteen hundred years before. After all, monasteries are not islands, and monastic life is influenced to a greater or lesser degree by the general social climate. But during the sixties a return to the old ways began, and the abbots gradually became the spiritual fathers of their communities again. Leadership in the monasteries has thus become more difficult, as it requires a very different kind of authority today, and some abbots give up. However, we have in this way once again come closer to

Benedict's idea of leadership, because while our founder rated the value of authority very highly, he thought very little of authoritarian structures.

What some people nowadays still find difficult even in our democratic times seems to have been obvious for Benedict: do not dispute the cleverness of others and be confident that everyone can also contribute useful ideas. In the third chapter of his Rule he says:

> As often as anything important is to be done in the monastery, the abbot shall call the whole community together and himself explain what the business is; and after hearing the advice of the brothers, let him ponder it. . . . The reason why we have said all should be called for counsel is that the Lord often reveals what is better to the younger.

To the younger! And that in an era when the reputation of a man was dependent on his age, when a young man's opinion counted for very little outside the monastery! One senses that Benedict feels the same dislike of routine and the daily grind as of the autocratic dealings of a superior. It is for this reason that he goes further and demands that the abbot should make no decisions even about minor matters before consulting the older brethren. In order to leave no one in any doubt about his "anti-authoritarian" attitude, he says finally, in his typical laconic style, "Do everything with counsel and you will not be sorry afterward."

It is particularly striking how remarkably progressive—or should we say how timelessly sensible?—Benedict's thinking is when we consider that for him the abbot is nothing less than the representative of Christ in the monastery. For Benedict he nevertheless remains a fallible man who, for all his wisdom and experience, can sometimes want for inspiration. What distinguishes the abbot from all others is his special responsibility but not his special relationship with God or greater grace or enlightenment. According to Benedict anyone could be inspired, from the humblest brother to Christ's representative in the shape of the abbot; the Spirit is not diluted on its way from top to bottom. What in our days still triggers hefty theological debates, the question as to whether the effect of the Holy Spirit is diminished by democratic processes, was apparently not a problem for Benedict. He simply connected both elements, the special gifts of the Spirit or authority of the abbot and the say of all the monks.

So collective leadership was my goal. I was not going to give up my authority, but I wanted everyone to feel responsible for the well-being of the community. Since then I have learned a lot: that everyone without exception wants to be considered; that you must talk to everyone who will be affected by something at an early stage and not just for form's sake; that you cannot imagine how easy it is for someone to feel left out; and that people at the lowest level of the hierarchy, and not only those in the higher echelons, have information no one else possesses. It's a hard path to follow, but it is the only one if the monastery is to become a dynamic place, a place where people can actually realize their ideals.

I think my experience at the monastery is in line with what has long been the general understanding of good leadership, that nothing is gained if the cart horse pulls powerfully and the wagon shaft breaks off behind it. In other words, all employees should be invited to share responsibility and everyone should have a say in all the processes that affect him or her personally. This sounds democratic, but it actually has nothing to do with democracy. This is not about codetermination, which often only serves to harden the fronts, but about participation, with the aim of fully exploiting the enormous potential of professional experience, imagination, and creativity that every employee, every team, and every working group presents. Another principle of wise leadership, as I see it, is that as a boss you must not isolate yourself. You must rather make every effort to involve the employees, first by keeping them up to date about all important events and developments, second by enabling them to participate in all the decisions that affect them, and third by sharing your responsibility with them.

"Our motto is 'Those who can, may,'" I was told by the legal advisor of a major bank. "Anyone with ability is allowed to show what he or she can do. Of course we have to be careful, of course we mustn't encourage megalomania. But I have had great success with assigning responsibility to young people at an early stage. We thrive on success, hence 'Those who can, may.'" Sharing power, assigning responsibility, involving everyone, automatically providing information: this is not a Utopian principle but a recipe for success. You can even reverse this motto to "Those who may, can," and it will still be applicable, because in many cases an employee will show herself capable of a demanding task when she is made to feel important. In order for this to happen, she must be supported not only in her field but as a person, because self-confidence must keep pace with the sense of responsibility.

The leader in turn must know that he needs the others. Sometimes, however, it takes time for him to realize that they are a help, not a hindrance or a nuisance factor. And not every manager is keen to involve his subordinates in the development of new ideas. It may be that he does not basically think them capable of producing clever ideas, but if this is so, his days as a leader are probably numbered. It may be that he is afraid of losing his authority if he has to acknowledge the independent achievements of his subordinates, but then his authority in any case leaves much to be desired. It may also be that he has had bad experiences with "creative" people; in that case he should ask himself whether perhaps he is not the cause. If a manager is really able to listen and allows true freedom of thought, grumbling and contrariness will soon subside of their own accord. So when I read that 80 percent of our managers prefer to rely on their own intuition and make lone decisions, I see a huge potential that can be put to use at no great expense.

I often find that managers are afraid their own opinions will not be heeded if everyone has her say. Before a meeting they worry about whether they will get their proposals through or fail because of the massive resistance of the others. For my part, at some point I said to myself that it did not matter in the end whether I won. I need the others, so I must see them as contributors and not as threatening, obstructive forces. This attitude works wonders, because it liberates in all participants the energy necessary to deal with a particular task. As soon as they sense my trust, the others lose all interest in a defensive battle. They then develop their own ideas because they realize these will meet with no resistance from me. There is no stronghold to be stormed, no ulterior motive to be exposed. All that matters is the topic in hand. And suddenly everyone is interested in constructive cooperation.

Here again it is a question of the extent to which a leader can take a backseat. The less she shows herself, the easier it is for her to integrate her people. A good leader must give every employee the feeling that he is not doing what this or that department head wants but what he himself wants and this goal is best achieved when a manager is inconspicuous, restrained, and unobtrusive. An egomaniacal boss from whom no one is safe, a manager who considers herself the linchpin of his department, not only destroys the self-esteem of her subordinates but also forfeits her own authority, and soon meetings become helpless disasters. One such scene featured an institute director who, after a tedious monologue in which he presented his views on the future of the institute, opened the floor for discussion and responded to the first critical remark by exclaiming pathetically, "This won't do! I can only use people who pull together!"

To illustrate the degree of sovereignty a cooperative management style requires, I would like once again to quote the legal advisor I mentioned earlier. "I had written a commentary on banking law," he told me, "and before publishing it I asked a colleague to tell me what she thought of my text. She read through it at home, then came to my office and started by flattering me. I stopped her. 'Please spare me that,' I said. 'I have the right to be criticized. And I am now claiming that right.' Gradually she came out with her criticism, and two-thirds of what she suggested I took to heart. So I expect honest opinions, because I can only benefit from honest opinions. When I realize that someone is only telling me what I want to hear, he gets transferred immediately."

You have already learned a lot about the art of leadership if you can rise above your weaknesses to this extent. Of course, it makes sense to involve your people, but that is not enough. As a boss you have to prove repeatedly how sincerely you are interested in creative and difficult employees. By this I don't mean grumblers or people who think themselves highly intellectual merely because they are always against something. Grumblers are never creative, and creative people are never grumblers. Grumblers may be present everywhere and at all times, but we should on no account use them as an excuse for making lone decisions. The wisest thing to do is discuss specific topics regularly in small groups in an atmosphere of trust where everyone can say what spontaneously occurs to him, where no one is intimidated and no one is ridiculed. That is the only way new ideas will be produced. Scarcely has one person thought of something than the next has another idea, the participants encourage each other, and, if the group is not too large, you can experience open, creative brainstorming, which can be an intellectual pleasure. And even if nine out of ten ideas are useless, it will have been worthwhile for the sake of the tenth.

I know it is not always easy to restrain yourself. It can be a major effort to ask for advice when you yourself do not feel the need of it. Nevertheless, you should first keep quiet about your own solution, even if you have long had it ready, and let the others speak first. The perplexity of a leader is a strong stimulus for those who are being led, because in this case they are not only acting out of objective necessity but are also doing you a personal favor. So never put your own ideas forward first: this crushes the others and freezes the discussion. It is much more important to try and draw them out. But not, of course, in order to mount a counterattack!

I often tell myself, "Wait until people think of it themselves. You can give them a helping hand, but you must not intervene from your position of authority." I might try opening their eyes, but I will not present them with a ready-made solution. I don't want to prove anything. What you yourself have discovered you treat as a treasure, as something important and precious, because it is associated with the pride of the discoverer and the happiness of discovery. To be shown or presented with something, on the other hand, is never remotely as gratifying, because you feel like a student who is obliged to listen to instruction that, even should it prove useful, will never mean as much as when you find something out for yourself. This, incidentally, applies not only to brainstorming but also to the practical carrying out of assignments. Those who execute orders should not feel burdened by their tasks. A wise manager should therefore set targets, define the framework, and provide the necessary information but not anticipate everything, not reveal too much and not interfere. Employees should be left to find their own way, because discoveries are a crucial element of work satisfaction. Let us repeatedly remind ourselves what a pleasure it is to concoct ideas, elaborate them and let them mature, and then experience how an idea becomes a plan, and the plan becomes a project and then a finished work. Suddenly you feel this wonderful productive restlessness, and in the end you grow a little more.

I find, by the way, that issues are sometimes better clarified by telling stories than by giving explanations, and conversations in smaller groups are often more profitable than public discussions. That's why I like getting away from the meeting atmosphere and the hierarchical conditions that put people under pressure to project themselves. In a restaurant, or on long car trips or walks, most people really open up. Suddenly it doesn't matter who has had which idea, because the thoughts can be allowed to flow without personal ambition getting in the way, and then something concrete emerges that sometimes seems wonderfully incidental. I would therefore advise managers to seek contact with their staff outside the offices and conference rooms. The more relaxed the situation, the better. You don't have to arrive at any decisions. But in this way ideas and projects ripen.

At some point, however, a decision must be made, and then there is an end to the discussions. A leader is expected to show strength and make it clear that the matter is closed. If serious errors of judgment are subsequently discovered, the course must naturally be corrected, but otherwise the original decision remains. One has not taken the easy way, and now there should also be no deviation from the hard-won position. Now it is the duty of managers to radiate confidence, to give moral support and provide protection. Employees need to feel assured that their boss is not weak-kneed. The vice-principal at our school in St. Ottilien was once asked in a meeting with the youth pastors, "Does the archabbot know what the youngsters at your school get up to?" "I've no idea," replied my vice-principal. "But if he did, I know he would back me up." I was, of course, glad that I did not always know everything.

Setting things in motion, encouraging, allowing people freedom—this is how I've always understood my role: not taking on everything myself but inspiring others, letting them concoct ideas and then adopting them, identifying opportunities, assessing the consequences, taking the initiative, and occasionally probing. I do not need to be involved in the implementation itself. At some point things have to run without my constant supervision. This does not mean I'm not interested, but others know and can do many things much better than I. That is how it always is: the higher you move up in the hierarchy, the more important your competence as a leader becomes and the more your particular expertise fades into the background. A person who has to manage half a dozen departments, from accounting to the legal and the tax sections, will inevitably understand less of a particular aspect than the respective professional. That is fine as long as he has the authority to follow things up with the specialist and say, "No, I don't understand, please explain it to me," instead of waving him away and saying, "Well, you do it, you're the expert."

Of course, leadership qualities cannot replace professional competence. The two go together, and they combine to particular effect when a manager has the ability to think outside the box: when she is not just content to see everything running as it should and functioning smoothly but foresees developments, seizes on promising ideas, and identifies new opportunities, in other words, cultivates visions. These need not be nocturnal inspirations. Visions can be ideas that have been picked up or read about somewhere and made one's own. They are not dreams. Visions are realistic and feasible, not ideals but goals, convincing enough to mobilize and inspire enthusiasm. If visions nowadays smack of utopia it is because the minimum consensus rules, because even the experts anticipate compromise in their reports and write only about what is possible and no longer about what is desirable, and because everywhere people think in terms of not being made liable. How infinitely enriching, however, to see a person with vision and have the rare pleasure of having to deal not with the person but with his or her thoughts! To my mind anyway, visionaries are the real energy center of a company—provided they do not stubbornly develop their ideas by themselves behind closed office doors. A vision can only be kept alive if many people share it.

As far as I and my Order are concerned, we are at a turning point. We are having to cope with the globalization of the Benedictine Order. The monasteries in the poor countries are growing while those in Europe are shrinking. What does this mean for the managerial staff at Sant' Anselmo? What paths should we follow in order to ensure the unity of the Order in future, to preserve the character of our Benedictine monasteries in so many different cultural contexts? Sant' Anselmo is the only institution of our Order that can promote and maintain this unity, as the various Benedictine monasteries are autonomous, independent units, and not even the abbot primate is authorized to issue instructions to the abbot of a monastery. If he wants to achieve something he must not just have convincing ideas, he must be convincing as a person as well, and his influence on the Order extends only as far as the trust that is placed in him. In other words, the Order as a whole is dependent on the understanding and voluntary solidarity of our communities around the world if we want to realize our plans and provide teacher training for as many students as possible from the monasteries of the Third World at the University of Sant' Anselmo and if we want to ensure that the university has the best staff and optimal financial support for the benefit of our monasteries in the long term. That, in any case, is our goal; that is our vision.

In recent times we have come closer to achieving this goal, and the way in which it happened will serve as the final example of how important it is to integrate all participants. Sant' Anselmo had previously had only very limited means at its disposal—the costs of the long-overdue repair of our roof alone exceeded our entire annual budget. In order to put Sant' Anselmo on a new financial footing, we felt it was essential to win the support of the prosperous North American abbeys for our vision. The problem was, however, that hardly anyone in the United States knew of our existence, and most of the American abbots had previously shown very little interest in Sant' Anselmo. Rome was just too far away, on the other side of the big pond and literally beyond their horizons. How could we get them to take responsibility for Sant' Anselmo and make our cause their own?

I succeeded in winning the support of my friend Archabbot Douglas for our vision. He presides over the Abbey of St. Vincent, the largest Benedictine monastery in the United States, and is an experienced fundraiser: for the needs of his abbey and university alone he maintains two development offices with a large staff. It was his idea to set up a separate office for Sant' Anselmo in the United States, to employ professional fundraisers, and to initially raise the half million dollars in annual maintenance costs from the American monasteries. Then it was up to me.

I traveled to the United States again and again. I explained to the American abbots what the situation was at Sant' Anselmo, what we were doing, and how important this place was for the future of the Order. I talked about the fellowships required so that our university could train students from poor countries to be teachers and professors and educate the next generation of leaders for the church all over the world. I spoke about the necessary renovation of the old building on the Aventine Hill and explained why it was worthwhile to make sacrifices for it. Later on I repeated my lecture to private individuals whose curiosity about our work had been aroused by some of the five thousand circulars produced by Archabbot Douglas. And suddenly the American abbots were interested in us. At last there was a basis of trust on which we could build closer cooperation. And at some point the first checks came in. Today it looks as if we are going to have a solid pillar of support in America. With this we are getting closer to realizing our vision. But before that happens I will probably be traveling to the United States many more times and drumming up enthusiasm for Sant' Anselmo, because it can be years before a foundation of this nature fulfills its intended purpose.

CHAPTER 5

Do Not Fear the Strong Man

On False and True Leaders

Abbot Primate Notker Wolf

Some time ago the head of the Bavarian state parliament asked me to conduct a weekend seminar for young politicians on leadership qualities and social responsibility. "Many of our young politicians today see no connection between leadership and responsibility," he said. "In the past it was different. Then most of our members were from a Catholic milieu and had already learned to take responsibility in Catholic parish youth groups. But there are not many of those left."

I of course knew what he meant. I had experienced myself that in rural communities the church had more to offer than Sunday masses. For us the church was part of home. There was a stronger emotional connection to the church community than to the political world, but as a young person you still got a foretaste of what we might call political *eros*, the joy of responsibility for people, for society as a whole, because when you were involved in these youth groups you automatically took responsibility. We learned so much!—keeping a cash book, preparing for group sessions, organizing a camp, maintaining discipline in the camp, etc. It was an honor to be part of this and a point of honor not to embarrass oneself. In this way the young people of that time developed a sense of responsibility without even thinking about it, and if they later ran for mayor or the district administration office they had a natural, credible authority.

After 1968 interest in the church and in attending services waned, and gradually the parish groups lost popularity. It is not least because of this development that the evolved sense of responsibility that represents true authority has become much rarer in the political and business world. Leadership is about taking responsibility for people because of your position, a responsibility that cannot be ignored except at the expense of those you lead. The later you learn this, the more difficult it is to do so. We will come back to this in a subsequent chapter in connection with school and education.

In addition to the individual reasons for poor leadership I have already talked about, in my opinion there are social causes as well. The decline of Christian youth work is certainly one of them. Another seems to me to be the widespread mistrust of the "strong man," our almost instinctive dislike of leaders who radiate power and self-confidence. This mistrust has become almost second nature, and at first glance it looks as if there is good reason for this: our own historical experience entitles us to feel this distrust, after all. At second glance, however, I find this reason rather unconvincing, and I shall explain why.

Most people today automatically associate the word "Führer" with the sinister figures of the twentieth century: Mussolini, Franco, Fidel Castro, and, of course, Adolf Hitler. They all called themselves leaders. Since then, in Germany the word "Führer" has no longer been socially acceptable, and even "Reiseführer" (guide-books) are now shamefacedly known by the English word "guides"; only "Führerschein" (driver's license) is still tolerated. Our image of a leader has been clouded to such an extent that in many areas of society we are missing out on the beneficial functions of a leader. I would therefore like to draw attention to the fact that there have been leaders other than the dictators of the twentieth century, first and foremost the great figure Moses, the archetypal leader and the model for heroes of freedom and civil rights activists like Martin Luther King, who also saw himself as a leader. The two types of leaders certainly have something in common: they all promised to lead their people to a better future. But we must not overlook the fundamental difference between them: the self-appointed leaders of the twentieth century in reality enslaved their people, while Moses actually led his people from slavery to freedom, and the journey through the desert was associated with a process of emancipation in the course of which the people learned how to deal responsibly with their new freedom. "Leader" does not mean the same thing in every case, and the execrated leaders I have listed did in fact lead their people astray. We should, instead, save the definition of "leader" for those who have courageously preceded their people on the path to freedom. Of these, Moses is the most charismatic example. Thus Martin Luther King based his hopes for the destiny of African Americans on the image of the people of Israel being led by Moses through the desert. Vatican II consciously drew on this picture when it described the church as the pilgrim people of God.

Of course, these leaders were powerful men. No one can deny that Mahatma Gandhi and Martin Luther King were impressive personalities, or say that the independence of India and the success of the civil rights movement in the United States would have come about had the leaders concerned been powerless men (or women). If "longing for the strong man" is still looked down on today, if we can hardly speak of masculine strength without it automatically being associated with pretension or arrogance, then we have become victims of a misunderstanding. We have mistaken strength for power and we are acting as if personal strength is as threatening as the concentration of power in a single individual. This is nonsense. Do we imagine we would be better served by powerless men? No movement can do without forceful men or women, and the antiauthoritarian movement of the sixties also gave us strong men in considerable numbers: we have only to think of student leaders such as Rudi Dutschke. Or there are models—although negative ones—such as Mao Tse-tung and Ho Chi Minh.

We should remember that leaders do not necessarily do terrible harm and strong men are needed every bit as much as strong women. We can be happy if our top executives are forceful men and women, quite apart from the fact that every business, every party, every political office needs a leader who can put flesh on a program, project, or the whole company.

The only question is thus how we want to define "strength." I would like to give three examples. The first concerns the exemplary function of the leader, the second the correlation between life experience and vital energy, and the third the willingness to be subject to control even when at the top.

Carrying out executive functions requires strength in part because others are watching what you do. A manager is constantly under observation, whether his subordinates are wary or admiring of him, and can be certain in any case that all eyes are on him. This is an enormous challenge. Everything he does or doesn't do has consequences; everyone knows when his behavior gives the lie to what he proclaims. He is always a model; he has no choice. But depending on the image he projects, he can either win or lose the loyalty of his subordinates. A person who overloads his employees with work, who expects them to stay on the job until late in the evening while he himself disappears at four o'clock in the afternoon because he is expected on the golf course, undermines his authority and will find, moreover, that every act of supervision will be interpreted as deliberate harassment. But the manager who does not spare himself, does not avoid conflicts, and carries out all his projects with total commitment will not only earn the respect of his employees but also encounter less resentment if something goes wrong. How seriously one takes one's function as role model is not just a question of personal morality but also a crucial aspect of wise leadership.

And it is anything but easy. My old prior's remark that eternally being a good role model was slowly killing him was thus not meant entirely as a joke. Some abbots also find it a burden to be constantly acting under the gaze of others. The only solution is to consciously view exemplary behavior as part of one's task. There is no way around it, because in everyday life virtues can only be taught by example. Abstract discussions about values of the kind that flare up from time to time in Germany, as in America, are totally worthless. Role models are what are needed, personalities who present values as a living culture. Authority must be experienced. The rest is palaver. Benedict also deems it necessary to point this out. In chapter two of his Rule he says:

[The abbot] must point out to them all that is good and holy more by example than by words, proposing the commandments of the Lord to receptive disciples with words, but demonstrating God's instructions to the stubborn and the dull by a living example. Again, if he teaches his disciples that something is not to be done, then neither must he do it.

And this is precisely how Lao Tzu had seen it around eight hundred years earlier. In the *Tao Te Ching* he wrote:

Therefore the wise embrace the One
   and become an example to all.
They do not display themselves and are therefore visible.
They do not justify themselves and are therefore great.
They do not make claims and are therefore given merit.
They do not seek glory and can therefore endure.

With this it should already be clear that someone who speaks in derogatory terms about the "strong man" has not understood either how great the challenge of leadership is or how much physical and emotional stress leaders are exposed to. Managers must be able to withstand a great deal, and this brings me to the second example. They are more likely to be able to do so the less often in their careers they have chosen the path of least resistance. In other words, in addition to all their other qualities, strong leaders have a lot of life experience. That experience is perhaps their greatest asset. People with textbook meteoric careers have little they can draw on when confronted with difficult situations. You should therefore never make things too easy for yourself. As a leader you must already have had the experience of coping with and surviving difficult situations. You should also be hardened to a certain extent against both criticism and flattery and not be knocked down too easily. It's best if you've had some ups and downs, been dealt blows and suffered setbacks, yet still found the courage to expose yourself to the unpredictable and incalculable.

In addition, in risky situations you train your intuition, sharpen your perception, and develop skills useful for dealing with a crisis.

The person who has avoided life is also unqualified to be a leader, precisely because she is underdeveloped emotionally. Here an incident comes to my mind that dates back many years. Shortly before my election as archabbot in St. Ottilien, an old confrère took me aside and said, "So, Reverend, are you healthy?"—"Well," I said, "more or less. In my childhood I was often ill, and later I got better. But I know what a hospital looks like from the inside." "That's good," he said. "An abbot should not be too healthy, otherwise he will have no sympathy for the weak and sick." This took me somewhat by surprise. I had never looked at it like that before. But the old confrère was right. Someone who has already seen the world from below is more likely to have the necessary empathy than someone who has gone through life unscathed.

Another product of life experience that should be mentioned here is knowledge of human nature. As a leader you have to respond to non-verbal signals; you must be able to see, for example, that this person is a troublemaker, that one will down sails at the first signs of a headwind, and this other one has his eye on the top position—and to do so you need the kind of intuition that develops with experience. If someone comes to me and wants to be accepted into the monastery, after ten minutes at most I can tell whether or not he is suitable for the monastic life. If I feel that someone is anxious about himself and yearning for recognition, I know he will not be happy with us, for we will never be able to provide him with the hoped-for self-affirmation. Our confrères have to be pretty independent; we are not a soft or "cuddly" Order. It is less a question of judging people by external signs than of sounding out their basic attitude, and for this a fair amount of life experience is necessary.

How little this has to do with power and how much with personal strength, with a knowledge of human nature and the vital energy nourished by rich experience! Again it shows how silly it is to automatically associate the idea of a "strong man" with power plays or omnipotent posturing.

With the third example I would like to remind you that strength can also be expressed in a very different way: through wise self-restraint rather than the triumphant bearing of the autocrat.

Of course, a leader must know what she wants. She should have at least a general line and be able to define goals. This is one of her most fundamental tasks and the way in which she justifies the basic trust of her staff. The person who does not know what she wants provides no orientation and is therefore not suitable as a leader. And however restrained and willing to cooperate the leader is, it must still be clear who is in charge and bears the responsibility. It would be a capital error to bashfully deny one's authority or perhaps hide in the group and plead the collective vote, according to the motto "That's what they all wanted. I was not in favor, but I was powerless in the matter." It is just as cowardly to defend decisions on the basis of scientific analysis or the reports of experts when common sense would suffice perfectly for assessing a particular matter. You should thus under no circumstances give the impression of shying away from the consequences of your responsibility. However, situations can arise in which it is advisable to submit voluntarily to greater control, and I found myself in just such a situation after my election as abbot primate in Sant' Anselmo.

My predecessor had placed a high value on having as free a hand as possible. I, on the other hand, wanted to decide nothing of importance on my own. I wanted to create an advisory body such as had not existed in this form before. Although my confrères thought a council of this nature would be unnecessary—which was certainly a sign that they trusted me—when I looked at the scale of the whole Sant' Anselmo complex and saw what burdens the various tasks of an abbot primate would place on me, I had to request this council.

An abbot primate is responsible first for the university and the abbey of Sant' Anselmo; in other words, he is the abbot of all the monks who live there during their studies and at the same time the boss of a growing number of employees who are organized in a wide variety of unions, as is typical in Italy. Second, he is responsible for the Order as a whole, which, among other things, means encouraging the individual monasteries to cooperate and preserving the unity of the whole Benedictine Confederation. This unity is not based on a specified structure; the abbot primate is, as it were, the missing link between the individual monasteries and must maintain relationships between them through personal contact. How an abbot primate fulfills his task is always a question of interpretation and discretion, and each one has to come up with something new. My idea, in any case, was to enter into a permanent exchange of ideas with all the monasteries, and that is why I needed the council—as a controlling and supporting body so that I would not be overwhelmed by my daily work.

So I founded this "Council of the Abbot Primate" and staffed it with leading members of Sant' Anselmo and representative members of the Order. The council supports me in dealing with personnel and financial issues and enables me to keep a constant check on our economic situation, but there is more to it than that. It also gives the others the assurance that their abbot primate is not doing anything arbitrarily and it is thus a very persuasive trust-building measure; likewise, it saves me from wrong decisions and short-sightedness, hence making my work much easier. In addition, the council members provide me with a good link with the monasteries in their home areas, which ultimately results in an increased interest in Sant' Anselmo. All in all, this council has proved a blessing, and when it was pointed out to me two years later that nothing of the kind was specified in our statutes and that the council was actually illegal, I took no notice. I needed this particular form of voluntary self-control. The council prevents unilateral action, and on top of this it represents a significant improvement in our problem-solving procedure, so we have retained it thus far without including it in the statutes. I do not want to leave my successor a legacy he might perhaps see as limiting his freedom to act. He might then feel constrained and only apply himself half-heartedly to his work; who knows? The council has thus remained to this day a tried and tested provisional arrangement.

I hope these three examples will suffice to show how absurd it is to immediately associate masculine strength with destructive forces. At the same time I see them as an appeal for a positive, relaxed attitude to authority. The latter is especially important for me. I believe that we need to develop a feeling for the humane, humanizing power of authority once again if leadership is not to amount to a choice between the arbitrary exercise of power and submission to a meticulous, politically correct code of behavior. Once we realize what makes up the strength of a leader, we might find it easier to arrive at an objective understanding of authority, free of the general suspicion of arrogant presumption. In one respect, however, I find distrust of the strong man justified: I am never quite comfortable when I witness the effect of charismatic leaders, as in such cases there is a danger that people can be led astray. Those who succumb to fascination will, at least temporarily, not be able to think clearly.

By this I am not trying to deny that we need people who charm, inspire, and fascinate, who are capable of achieving great things due to their charisma and power of attraction. Sometimes, however, I have experienced people following a charismatic person too passively for my liking. Perhaps I'm overly skeptical in this respect, but even during my last visit to Frère Roger Schütz at Taizé I was momentarily disturbed. Frère Roger, undoubtedly a great charismatic person and equally above all suspicion, was leaning against a pillar because of his advanced age, and the young people who had attended the service sitting on the ground now formed a long queue, went down on their knees, and shuffled up to him to receive his blessing individually. I was deeply impressed by this picture of complete devotion—and simultaneously I was momentarily disconcerted by the state of trance in which they seemed to find themselves.

As I said, there was never any danger of manipulation with Frère Roger. For me he was the epitome of a blessed charismatic leader who directed the attention of the young people flocking to him away from his person and toward God. He showed us what makes people truly charismatic: they do not try to get people under their sway and are not carried away by their own charisma. We should therefore always consider whether people with a great presence combine their ability to inspire and convince people with practical common sense and self-control. Frère Roger, Mother Teresa, Nelson Mandela, and Martin Luther King have passed this test in my eyes.

There is one problem, however, that arises from the very nature of the situation and is therefore hard to get a handle on: what happens when a charismatic leader retires; who is to succeed him or her? Charismatic people cannot, after all, really be replaced, and often the work stands and falls with the person who has made a success of it. Roger Schütz had the foresight to name his own successor, and he thus spared his community an ordeal. Successful leaders often neglect to settle this matter and would rather hazard the failure of their work than run the risk of falling victim to the ambitions of a successor. They fail to recognize that it is the last and highest duty of every leader to make himself redundant. I have thus always made sure that the most able of my people receive excellent training and are placed in responsible positions as soon as possible so that they can take my position at any time. However, there is no guarantee in the Order that any of these "crown princes" will actually become my successor, because the community elects the abbot, and their choice may fall equally on any other person. Nevertheless, I still prefer to know that I'm replaceable.

CHAPTER 6

Leaders Must Be Artists

What I Expect from a Manager

Sister Enrica Rosanna

Abbot Primate Notker calls the Rule of St. Benedict an endless source of inspiration for all who are faced with the question of how to lead people and how to organize life in a community—quite rightly, in my opinion. Although the Benedictine Rule does not determine my life to the same extent as his—I am a Salesian, and unlike the Benedictines we have not chosen life in a cloistered community—I experience the validity of this Rule as a universal standard, as it were. The pope has assigned responsibility for monasteries to me, and I can confirm that St. Benedict really is the father of the religious life. What he writes is simple and concrete; it shows an extraordinary inner balance and can therefore provide orientation for all religious communities.

I should probably say that my experience with the many different Orders is not confined to the cases I handle from my desk here in the Vatican. When difficult problems arise I often involve the abbot, the abbess, or a sister so that we can look for a solution together. I also travel to meet in person with the people who have asked us for help, because with complex problems I can only bring my pastoral experience to bear by talking from woman to man or woman to woman and not by telephoning or through written correspondence alone. Sometimes I travel for training purposes or to give lectures, and then there is often an opportunity to talk to abbots or abbesses about their roles or the particular difficulties of the individual Orders in the world today. Some of them are over-burdened; some things have gone wrong, and I hear about many of the problems and conflicts firsthand.

I always endeavor to fulfill my duties in the spirit of Christianity, and although in this book I am writing about leadership in the broadest sense, the qualities of a Christian leader seem to me to be the most solid basis for good leadership. So I will start with the image of a leader who is more than head of a company, who does not lead merely in a sociological sense but through his faith brings the values of Christianity such as peace, justice, and harmony into politics, the economy, and individual enterprises as well as into schools and families. It is just such people I feel are in short supply today. Christianity is not something private; it is public because it affects everything that human beings are and do. The happiness of the individual and the general good therefore in my opinion depend on our acquiring these values that are the heritage of Christianity and putting them into practice in society.

We are not just doers; we also have a being. For me as a religious leader this means that the task entrusted to me has to be a vocation. It must not be merely a role I play or work I do; it must instead become the highest expression of myself so that I can give not only all my energy but everything I am as a human being. It is not enough, therefore, for me to show myself proficient in what I would call the art of governing, conscientiously and effectively solving all the problems that are brought to my attention. I must also master what I understand as the art of encouraging, stimulating, and awakening powers so that I can help the people I am dealing with to live in accordance with their mission and identity. What is sometimes difficult is balancing these two arts within yourself, or, in other words, sensing which situation requires an objective solution in accordance with the art of governing and which requires personal intervention in the sense of the art of encouraging.

In any case, as leaders we have to be artists. By art, however, I do not mean striving for unattainable perfection. An artist, in my view, is rather someone who constantly develops and expands the skills his or her job requires. Looked at in this way, an artist is nothing special, and religious leaders, at least, are all expected to be artists whether with respect to prayer, suffering, or fulfilling their responsibilities. Not everyone, certainly, has the ability to lead. Some people are entirely unsuitable for leadership roles—as unsuitable as I am to be a cook, for example. I cannot cook, and I do not want to learn, because I know that is not one of my talents. However, if a person has leadership qualities, he cannot just sit back and rely solely on his charisma, his innate authority. He must constantly work on himself; he must adapt, expand, develop, and internalize his aptitudes and skills. This is alluded to by St. Catherine of Siena when she says, "Be what you ought to be—and you will revolutionize Italy. Continue to learn about what you already know. Make constant improvements to what you do and what you are." Starting out as a leader is like embarking on a marriage: when two people get married they are husband and wife, but they have not yet learned what it means to be husband and wife because they have no experience of it. Everything has to prove itself in practice in the course of life, has to grow and mature with time.

So what skills help us to constantly improve in our role as leaders? I would like to mention three. The first is prudence. For me it is a cardinal virtue, and a very difficult one. Prudence is an expression of human maturity. It requires an inner balance that many people only develop gradually, but rarely to such perfection that they do not repeatedly have to struggle to maintain it. When my inner balance is threatened I always think of a Madonna statue in a small town just outside Rome; it is the Madonna of equilibrium, of calmness, and there is no festival in her honor simply because she is invoked from morning till night. She is certainly one of the most popular Madonnas of all, and we would undoubtedly do well to put ourselves under her care. In other words, prudence and calm are both worth every effort, just because as a leader you never should improvise or rush into anything. Impetuosity and haste ruin the best intentions, and anyone who lets herself get carried away by her own emotions can cause incalculable damage. Even under the greatest external pressure we must not react violently, and if ever we really do lose control of ourselves we must have the courage to start all over again and also to ask for forgiveness. Moreover, we will be even more prudent if we accustom ourselves to making no absolute judgments and not insisting on being absolutely right at any price.

The second gift that distinguishes a leader is patience. As children of this society we are in a permanent hurry. We increasingly want immediate results and rush to change programs and methods if the hoped-for success is not immediately apparent. But a hectic boss cannot lead. He must understand that everything takes time and results will only materialize at the rate that a person grows and matures. He probably has to learn to have patience with himself first of all before he can leave others alone. That does not mean taking it easy. He should take an interest in how others are coping. Patience never means leaving subordinates to their own devices—it is, after all, one of the most important tasks of leaders to ensure the cohesion of a community, because there will otherwise be a growing number of conflicts. And then we also need patience, because as managers and educators we must be expert listeners. Many people are great talkers, but few are great listeners; however, the right word is always born of careful listening. Personally I must, for example, keep reminding myself that behind many of the documents I work through every day are individual people with their pain and personal tragedies, so that I listen in each file to hear what these people are really saying.

The third gift is courage. Woe betide the leader who has no courage! We must recognize that leadership culture is based to a large extent on courage, if only because managers and educators must always make it clear what is in order and what is not, so that they can change course if necessary. Lack of courage is often disguised as tolerance or equanimity when in reality the leader only wants her peace and dares not correct errors and address shortcomings. We must, however, behave exactly as we expect others to and have the courage to criticize ourselves. No one is perfect, and no one is expected to be perfect. But everyone must know that she must not resign herself to her faults. The founder of my religious institute, Maria Domenica Mazzarello, expressed it thus: "You do not have to be perfect, but you must not make peace with your faults."

Of course, a leader needs courage in order to resolve conflicts. She is responsible for peace in the community and must therefore know how to settle disputes and intervene before petty frictions become out-and-out war, with everyone on one side or the other. But it also takes courage to accept that we cannot put an end to every conflict—nor should we always try to do so, because the art of leadership consists not least in showing others how to live with conflicts and learn from them. Conflicts are part of life, and reconciliation does not necessarily have to be the first thing that occurs to us the minute there is an angry outburst. Certainly we must not tolerate undesirable developments that bear the seeds of discord, but if I do not allow any tensions to exist, do not accept any challenges, and run away from anything that might hurt, I will never grow or progress as a person. I have learned so much myself from conflicts with fellow sisters or confrères, and I have benefited so many times from the painful experience of having someone tell me the truth to my face! Let us therefore not take the easy way out with respect to conflict. Let us not overlook what is going wrong out of cowardice or ignore what could be beneficial for us because we are afraid of conflict.

These principles of good leadership must, of course, be lived out and embodied by the leader. It is then that one's character and temperament, as well as one's education, come into play. I believe my own character makes it easier for me to cope with my responsibilities, which, as I said, primarily involve not technical procedures but human lives. I find it relatively easy to make contact with others; I am quite sociable and above all not easily offended. I fail to hear insults, or I forget them immediately. None of this is my doing. I come from the north of Italy, from Lombardy, and while we Lombards are temperamental, we also calm down just as quickly as we get worked up. Here my origins serve me in good stead. And should it happen that I really cannot forgive an offense, I go down on my knees and pray.

There are also things that can be learned. For example, I owe a lot to the very intensive cultural education I received, which refined and reinforced some of my talents, and also to my years of teaching experience. At synods foreign bishops often said to me, "Sister, when you speak, I understand everything." Well, I did teach for many years, which accustoms you to structuring your presentations logically and being aware that your listeners too need a theme they can follow.

I would like to conclude this chapter by pointing to two really impressive examples of good management: the emeritus pope, Benedict XVI, and his predecessor, Pope John Paul II. The latter was undoubtedly the pope of fellowship with people, of rapport and understanding across all boundaries and of hope and passion. Young people in particular saw him as an ally and companion because he had a genuinely sympathetic ear for them, because he fired them with an enthusiasm that overcame all difficulties, and because he was simultaneously able to provoke, challenge, and make demands. About Pope Benedict, on the other hand, people were initially skeptical. We asked ourselves how he would be able to follow in the footsteps of his predecessor and how someone so shy would conquer the hearts of men and women.

But then it became clear that with economical means Benedict XVI was achieving the same as John Paul II. The window of my office overlooked St. Peter's Square, which in recent years was filled for the Sunday Angelus as never before. This person who formerly seemed so stiff and aloof turned out to be accessible and straightforward. For me Benedict is today the pope of clarity, sincerity, moderation, and balance, and I think that these last two popes complement each other wonderfully. Benedict gave the great visions of John Paul depth and content, and thus fulfilled the most important requirements of a leader: he gave those he led clear orientation.

CHAPTER 7

It Is Said That . . .

How to Deal with Crises and Defuse Confrontations

Abbot Primate Notker Wolf

Like all big businesses, we also have various power centers, and it is precisely the promising people who fall victim to the struggle between them. So if power center A furthers a particular person, power center B does what it can to undermine him or her. It hardly ever happens that the two centers ask themselves whether this man or this woman is suitable for the job in question. All that matters is whose orbit you are in, whose battalion. And then the only question is which battalion is the strongest. Achievement is secondary.

It was thus that a person from middle management described the power struggles in his company. It is no different when we hear about the tensions behind the scenes of a major concern, or when Edzard Reuter, the former head of Daimler-Benz, describes in his memoirs how much energy was wasted in his company through power struggles and turf wars. It is no coincidence that managers often use vocabulary taken from the language of the military. The talk is of shooting down and firing back, and the martial terminology merely disguises the fact that the scene of such carnage is simply the carnival with which some people in leadership positions confuse their companies. "We don't talk about leaders in terms of personality," added the man I quoted at the beginning, "but in terms of power. Power counts, personality doesn't." It may well be that in many places the situation is not as dramatic as this, but it cannot, after all, be denied that where money, prestige, and influence are at stake, favoritism prevails, intrigues are played out, and jealousy and malice are the order of the day; my first piece of advice is therefore to live with the fact that not every colleague or employee is pursuing altruistic goals.

Many people, especially of the younger generation, find this realism difficult. The harmonious world sought by those who refuse to see malevolence anywhere is one of the most treasured illusions of our day. The problem with this wishful image, however, is that troublemakers have to be demonized as ideological opponents or enemies of humanity, which does nothing to further the cause of peace. This is why for me another principle of wise leadership is to endure tensions and deal with conflicts so that problems between individuals don't immediately result in a split or a breakdown. In other words, power struggles must be avoided—or weathered. A leader who fails to confront this issue loses her authority. People of sound intuition will be aware of it immediately if someone is shying away from confrontations, and may possibly earmark her as a victim. If we are therefore forced to struggle for power we should not back down. But we should also never descend to the level of people who operate undercover! It does not have to be like this. I have had good experience of undermining power struggles and thwarting an opponent's game by displaying a disarming openness.

Intriguers are most likely to give up when they realize that all their tricks can be seen through, and they should be told this in a frank, private discussion. If somebody tries to trick or set a trap for you, make the effort to talk to him and make it clear that he is not going to gain any advantages. Say to him, "This will get neither of us anywhere. You are damaging not only me but also yourself." I am convinced that honesty is the best policy, even in such cases. Admittedly, discussions with devious people are not pleasant. But as the person who does not need to resort to dirty methods you hold the trump card and are therefore in a stronger position. And in this way you also reinforce your own credibility, which is an invaluable asset precisely in conflict situations.

Every power struggle is basically a betrayal of the corporate goal, which is why such disputes should be ended as soon as possible with a fair offer of cooperation. But even when all you have to offer in tricky situations is your own sincerity you will often find a solution. I myself, at least, have tackled the most problematic cases in this way and have ultimately been successful.

To give just one example of this: it sometimes happens that the abbot and his monastery are divided. I am thinking here of a very capable abbot whose only failing was that he considered everyone else incompetent. By playing a lone hand he forfeited the solidarity of his confrères, and one day he was accused of financial irregularities. I went into these allegations and, although they were unfounded, I understood the resentment of his monks: he was simply not acting wisely. He was too self-assured; he thought he was the abbey. I visited him, talked to him in private, suggested he resign, and said to him: "Maybe you're right. Maybe some of the accusations made against you actually have no foundation, but things have gone so far that the question of who is right is no longer important. It's not possible to patch things up anymore. At this stage there is no going back. . . ." It was a painful duty. When you know someone well, as was the case here, it is much more difficult to tell him unpleasant truths than if you are only distantly acquainted. Finally, after a long discussion, he resigned with a heavy heart but perhaps a little wiser.

Honesty is the best policy. It may come as a surprise that this saying is also applicable to the everyday world of a manager. I too have learned over time to tell others unfailingly what I think, not in a brutal manner but gently; it is a basic principle I always apply. I think it is wrong to hem and haw and make vague allusions in the hope that the other person will get the point himself. I am not doing him any favors by leaving him "mercifully" in doubt, and I am doing myself no service by fooling someone. Credibility is ultimately and in every case the most convincing argument, and it is understood worldwide. In the years of negotiations that preceded the construction of our first hospital in China, I also strictly followed the principle of laying my cards on the table and of arguing in such a way that my reasons were always comprehensible. Back in the nineties hardly anyone apart from me believed in the success of these negotiations—especially since we wanted to establish this clinic as a joint venture, with Benedictine participation both in the construction and the management, which met with considerable resistance from the Chinese. And yet today this hospital exists; it went into operation in 2001 and is jointly managed by Chinese and Benedictine sisters. This would never have come about if my Chinese negotiators had not been firmly convinced of the sincerity of my intentions.

However, I must concede that I can imagine situations in which this does not apply. It seems to me entirely justified to ask whether one should feel obliged to be as honest in the public setting of meetings and conferences as in a small group of negotiators or employees.

It's true that every internal conference may boil down to a test of courage. The person who makes an objection twice in one morning goes down on record. Do you then say openly what you think in spite of this? And how often can you afford to be so candid without risking your career? Or is it better to hold back as long as no other colleague is pulling in the same direction? For many members of middle management this is an ongoing problem, but it is no different on boards of directors or in cabinets: the person who stands out through dissent is considered unreliable and risks being put on the hit list. I cannot therefore advise anyone to make a martyr of herself, but I think prospects are poor for the company that expects its employees to show heroic courage in the face of controversy. The extent to which unpleasant issues can also be aired in public is for me the best measure of a humane working environment, the key indicator of the anxiety-free space I talked about in the third chapter. That space will not be produced by laying down minimum standards of human interaction and practicing humanity "by the book." It requires leaders who are strong enough to have their defensive and offensive reflexes under control.

It is in our nature that in critical situations alarm bells go off before we use our heads. And then it is quite irrelevant how minor the cause is, whether you are, for example, only annoyed because you didn't put forward the crucial solution at the right moment yourself: this is already enough to make you feel a loser and create an underlying sense of anxiety, and the primitive survival instinct in all of us kicks in with a counterattack or defensive behavior— reflexively, in a fraction of a second. I know this: some of our Order's superiors too are very quick to feel attacked, harassed, or driven into a corner, and I am by no means a stranger to a feeling of uneasiness and displeasure if resistance comes from an unexpected quarter. In most people a whole array of vanities, ambitions, fears, and personal animosities is activated in such situations, and when we are startled out of our self-confidence there are only two natural reactions: letting off steam or taking cover, sulking in a corner or retreating to your bunker.

The person who decides for the bunker is closed to her coworkers and colleagues; she may shut herself off completely and try, as it were, to rule against the rest of the world. This will inevitably harden the fronts. I remember such a case in one of our abbeys. There the abbot made the mistake of going it alone and responded with high-handed obstinacy to criticism. The community wanted him to submit to stronger control and in every election voted against the declared will of the abbot and in favor of candidates who would defy him. The abbot was thus sidelined. But so was the whole abbey. Things went neither forward nor backward, which caused endless frustration on both sides. The sulkers, on the other hand, as I see it, are bosses who hide behind formalities when there is a conflict. They become authoritarian, trumpet their power and authority, demand loyalty and obedience, and even on occasion request oaths of allegiance and vows of submission. When cornered they set up a protective area, a *cordon sanitaire* around themselves that no one may enter because, having become aware of their vulnerability, they don't want anyone to come too close. But even that is no help. As soon as you become entrenched behind your authority you are lost. While the mere authority of office is necessary to ensure a minimum of functionality, for someone who relies on it as a last resort it has the same disadvantage as the emperor's new clothes.

In crisis and conflict situations there is thus only one solution: We must control our natural reflexes. This means that personal vulnerability must not play a role at all. Here we come back to the problem we already discussed in the second chapter, namely, anxiety about ourselves, the anxiety that makes us resort to irrational strategies of self-assertion, makes us blind to the requirements of the moment and unfit for leadership. How can we overcome this fear?—by not relying on the pseudo-solutions of power that liberate us from dependence on others by making us insensitive to their feelings and needs. The only real solution is an inner conversion that will liberate us from dependence on ourselves while making us keen eared, perceptive, and sensitive to the reactions of others and the demands of our task. This repentance and renunciation of oneself is what I think Sister Rosanna means by the art of leadership: the continuous practice of detachment from oneself and closeness to others. The ultimate goal of this long process would be reconciliation with oneself, and the result would be called sovereignty.

What does that mean? I would define sovereignty as greatness manifested as modesty, as strength expressed as empathy and understanding, and as the inner freedom to defer one's own concerns and be of service. Sovereignty is, strictly speaking, the central concept of this book and basically also the main idea behind any form of leadership not founded on power. Sovereignty enables us to respond appropriately in all situations in which controlled action is required; it helps us above all to resolve and deal properly with conflicts so that they don't leave an unpleasant aftertaste. I would now like to take a brief look at a few such situations.

In principle, the authority of a good manager is sufficient by itself to prevent conflicts or nip them in the bud because authority has a calming effect, and the presence of a strong character smoothes the waters before troubles have a chance to develop. Ultimately, a community or a team is no different from a child who calms down immediately when he feels the presence of his mother in the house. He does not even have to see her. The presence of an authority figure always provides security. I also notice this in our monasteries: if the abbot is present there is automatically a calmer atmosphere.

People will always grumble, stir things up, whisper behind others' backs, cavil and spread rumors. In the long run that is harmful to a community; Benedict was therefore practically allergic to what he called murmuring. As a manager you have two options for dealing with this: either ignoring it if it is just a momentary upsurge of resentment or idle talk that will be forgotten the less you make of it, or taking up the matter the minute you hear about it. It may be that the usual communication channels were not functioning properly and people had legitimate questions. In that case they are only to be blamed if they didn't turn to those who could immediately provide information but preferred instead to make the wildest presumptions and become suspicious. At the earliest opportunity I take the mutterers aside and say, "It's being said that . . ."—and the subject is thus broached without anyone feeling attacked.

Particular attention should be paid to the development of mistrust. It is often difficult to locate it; you have to develop a knack of sensing it wherever it arises. Once located, it should be tackled without hesitation, before mistrust turns into concrete opposition and causes a leadership crisis. It is not always easy to address a general sense of mistrust and be so objective about it that nobody will misinterpret it as an attack. I try opening the topic with the words, "I have the impression that not everyone agrees . . ." or "We don't seem to have come to an entirely satisfactory conclusion." It could well be that even after a prolonged debate there is still something that has not been resolved, or perhaps there is growing animosity that must first be dealt with and the time is in fact not yet ripe for a decision. The sooner a boss is willing to consider factual causes for existing mistrust, the less he is in danger of relating them to himself. He thus saves himself unnecessary aggravation.

Of course, as a boss you always have to consider whether it is advisable to intervene or wiser to turn a blind eye. You must not be governed by convenience, let alone cowardice. It's easy to let things drag and it is cowardly to let employees play computer games during working hours; neither course of action will contribute to a humane climate. Both a people-friendly working atmosphere and the authority of the boss depend on the fact that the rules cannot be questioned at will. As well as being able to sense when liberality is appropriate and when intransigence is required, you must have the courage to speak openly with the employees when you detect a change in the atmosphere or sense a feeling of resentment. If someone has actually done something wrong, you must have not only courage but self-control. The biggest mistake then would be to use the opportunity to dress down the guilty party or parties. The cardinal rule in this case is not to add human damage to the damage done to the company. It is so important for St. Benedict that abbots follow this principle that he repeats it frequently, as, for example, in chapter 64 of his Rule, which states: "He should always *let mercy triumph over judgment.* . . . By this we do not mean that he should allow faults to flourish, but rather, as we have already said, he should prune them away with prudence and love as he sees best for each individual."

You should thus avoid morally lambasting the guilty; a manager is never in any case entitled to do so. But you should also avoid going into the background of a particular mistake and tracing a disaster back to its origins. The past is really not important when there is a crisis to be managed. Only the actual situation is of interest, the condition that now prevails, however aggravating it is. It has happened. Now the facts have to be accepted and you have to proceed from them and not start any discussions in the vein of "Well, if this or that had not happened . . . ." "What's done is done," I say, "it's no use crying over spilled milk. All that is important is finding a way out of this mess." In short, in a crisis one requires a large measure of objectivity and self-control in order not to resort to accusations and the examination of causes but to keep the matter at hand firmly in view. But this kind of discipline pays off. I was given an impressive example by someone in the upper management of a bank. "It often happened," he said, "that a branch manager made a major error, or a credit was lost. I then sent for the culprit and we jointly explored all the possibilities for saving what could be saved. Of course, I could have heaped reproaches on the man's head. I could have wiped the floor with him. But what would have been the point? If you want to make the best of a bad job, you need someone who can think clearly, and an intimidated person cannot do that. In this way I not only saved numerous careers, but we also usually succeeded in restoring order for the most part."

Unfortunately, care for the individual and concern for the company as a whole cannot always be so harmoniously combined, and as the leader you must always consider the extent to which you can accommodate an individual without alienating others or harming the company. Of course, every employee expects to be treated fairly, but as a manager you must know that in some cases you might be being unfair to everyone else by trying to be absolutely fair to a particular individual. I have often had to refuse a confrère something for the sole reason that it would have put the community under considerable strain. Benedict, incidentally, weighs up the interests of the individual and the community so minutely that he instructs his monks, for example, not to go into too much detail about their experiences after returning from a journey, because this could stir up the envy of those left behind and disturb the monastery's peace.

So far we have seen that a good sense of the general atmosphere, level-headedness in the case of a mishap, as well as courage and self-control are essential aspects of sovereignty. These virtues are of course required of a manager on an everyday basis, but they are primarily put to the test in meetings and discussions, as I will discuss in greater detail below. First, however, I would like to describe a particularly precarious situation I experienced as archabbot of St. Ottilien that was triggered by, of all people, my old prior.

The matter in question was the restoration of our abbey church, the most costly project of my tenure. After years of planning, the day of the chapter meeting at which the decision would be made had finally arrived, and my big worry was that the community could split in two, because approximately the same number of confrères were for it as were against it. I knew, at any rate, that my old prior was on my side. In the final discussion the majority seemed to my relief to be in favor of the plans that had been drawn up, and I wanted to put it to a vote. Then Prior Paul asked to speak. "Well," he said, "Actually this was how I also envisaged the renovation. But now I've come to the conclusion that it is better as it is. So I don't think we should change anything." I was flabbergasted.

What should I do? I had trained myself never to react to objections with anger or by shaking my head. I had learned to be grateful that direct objections were still being made in meetings. I had made sure that no opponent had to make the effort to break down my defenses. I had had good experience with ignoring gobbledygook and letting it go uncommented. I had also made it a rule to take even the most conceited person seriously and also to ask myself with the most stubborn opponents, "What is really his problem? What unsatisfied need for recognition is perhaps behind this?" And everyone could always expect a factual answer from me. But now? How should I respond to the fact that at the last minute my prior was trying with his brief statement to put a stop to such an important project? I controlled myself and said, "Father Prior, I respect your opinion; after all the previous discussions I myself am of a different opinion. But if some of you feel we haven't talked about this enough, I am willing to continue." At this point I was interrupted. "Certainly not!" exclaimed the others. "We have finished discussing the pros and cons. Now we are going to vote!" That was a weight off my mind. I looked at my prior. He cleared his throat and said, "Well, if we really want to renovate, then now rather than later because we currently have the necessary money. Who knows if we will still have it in the future." A further weight was taken off my heart. The renovation was approved. And my prior loyally supported it.

Skillful management of a discussion therefore involves bringing the others over to your side, with a bit of luck, even though they do not necessarily share your opinion. Unobjective and superfluous objections annoy everyone, and all the participants watch the chairman very carefully in such situations, curious to see how he will react; many hit the ceiling on his behalf when he keeps calm. He can then sit back. He must never show what he is feeling, because as a leader he primarily has to act as a mediator in the group, and, to put it plainly, keep things peaceful, so he must not look as if he is struggling to keep himself under control. In particular, he must allow his own views to be discussed as well as those of the others. In this way he creates an atmosphere of candor and encouragement—in other words, of creativity. Now it is possible to argue and represent one's position without running the risk of being morally or intellectually embarrassed. You can also hold the discussion with the confidence that everyone who is unable to control his hostility, his need to project an image, or his loquacity will make himself look ridiculous.

In meetings one must assume that many people are not aware of their motives at the moment when they make a statement. I therefore let self-promoters run on until they themselves notice with shame that they are on the wrong track. A dry, strictly factual remark is enough; often they feel caught out and at the same time embarrassed that they indulged their tendency to project themselves. I find people who just sit there and don't say anything more annoying. You don't know where you are with them and at some point start to feel unsettled. The best thing to do is to get them to talk. I speak to these people, challenge them—in an interested but never sarcastic tone—and I usually succeed in turning silent observers into real participants. The snipers and saboteurs are of course the most unpleasant of all. To cope with such people you need a knowledge of human nature and some wiliness, because you must sense or foresee what they are going to do or must be able immediately to see through them, which is why you must not be too trusting. Here the strategy is also to take the wind out of their sails, let them run on, thank them for their original contribution, or simply agree with them. Such people expect to encounter fierce resistance, or at least cause confusion, and they are disarmed if they instead meet with courtesy or understanding. Doing exactly what your opponent doesn't expect is a strategy I practiced successfully when I was at school. The whole class decided to counter the rebukes of our teachers not by trying to justify ourselves but rather by cheerful agreement. We thus regularly responded to outraged teachers by saying, "I'm sorry; you're right." This was like sticking a knife into a tire—and, of course, it was a particularly mean way of getting at the teachers . . . .

Incidentally, I have had good experience with appointing a moderator for large meetings. This is a simple but effective measure. I talk too much sometimes when I am committed to something and I am grateful when a moderator puts the brakes on. Another very simple and helpful method of self-control originates from Julius Caesar, who is said to have made it a rule to count to twenty before reacting. At the rate we proceed in working life today, we'd probably never get to twenty, but a conscious slowing down of one's reactions at critical moments is the best way of avoiding thoughtless or knee-jerk reactions. I can recommend practicing it. Many people will then discover that consciously delaying one's reactions is not at all easy—just try waiting only three seconds before answering. Even this can seem like an eternity.

Finally, a personal confession: no sovereign leader, as I see it, can be lacking in a sense of humor. I consider humor a reliable indication of the necessary distance from oneself and can therefore only agree with the abbot who said to me years ago, "If someone wants to enter our monastery, I first establish whether or not he has a sense of humor. I can teach him faith if need be, but not humor." It is undeniable that as managers humorous people are more relaxed and therefore better at their job, and they always have the advantage when it comes to taking the wind out of people's sails. I remember an experience I had with a monk of the old school in Rome when I was teaching at Sant' Anselmo. This confrère, very pious, a little cunning, and at the same time rather submissive, had caused my Fiat 127 to be stolen through his own negligence. I had given him a piece of my mind. In the evening at ten o'clock when I was sitting reading in my room, very lightly dressed because of the Roman heat, there was a sudden knock at my door. Perhaps it's a student, I thought, and said, "Come in!" The door opened, and my old, pious confrère entered the room, put on a very contrite expression, prostrated himself in front of me on the floor, and asked for my blessing. Well, I gave him the blessing and that was the end of that as far as I was concerned. But the scene was repeated the next day and the day after that. And when he was lying in front of me yet again on the fourth evening, I had had enough. "Well, my dear confrère," I said, "Now you're getting a punishment. I forgave you ages ago. But I forbid you ever to disturb me again in my sacred private sphere after Compline. Good night!" That ended the nightmare.

CHAPTER 8

Blessed the One Who Can Distinguish a Grain of Sand from a Mountain

On Praising, Criticizing, and Motivating

Abbot Primate Notker Wolf

It happened on a journey to South America. In one of the monasteries, at the end of a busy day, the principal of our school asked me to visit the newly renovated school building. But I did not want to. I had had enough. I said, "Please forgive me, but if you knew how many schools I have already seen on my journeys . . . I'm sure you've done a good job." And I counted on his understanding; we were old friends. I then noticed when we met on subsequent occasions that something was wrong. He was still friendly, but not in the same way as before. For three years he avoided my questions, but then he came out with it. I had hurt his pride. The renovated school building was not a status symbol for him, but a new beginning he had accomplished by his own efforts, and I had not been ready to appreciate this. I had made a mistake.

If someone has worked hard at something, she needs recognition. Everyone deserves this, from your best friend to the most arrogant of people. I should have known it. I remember only too well how encouraged I myself felt by the assurance of my old prior at the beginning of my tenure as archabbot. Before my first trip to Africa it was being said in the monastery that the new abbot traveled too much. Prior Paul took me aside and said, "Just go; the people there want to meet you." That did me good. And when, after my election, a confrère questioned my competence, Prior Paul said simply, "The election was legal, and Notker Wolf is our archabbot. Otherwise all our talk about the Holy Spirit is just nonsense." Even a leader relies on moral support—and to a much greater degree than a subordinate! Hence the next principle of wise leadership is that a boss must motivate her people to bold action through praise, recognition, and encouragement, as well as rebuking and criticizing them when necessary.

It is a sign of weakness when professional people in leading positions want to be left alone and are reluctant to leave the ivory tower of their acknowledged expertise: self-esteem is conveyed by language, and a boss must therefore be outgoing and associate with his people, must maintain contact and express professional and personal interest in them. In short, a person who wants to lead others has to master the art of conversation. Praise and criticism are the classic test of this art.

Enough has already been said about how much can be achieved through praise and recognition. Everyone is familiar with the fact that employees whose activities are noticed and appreciated don't look at the clock. I would like to remind managers who nevertheless find it extremely hard to praise that nothing is as motivating as merited praise, because it increases a person's pleasure in his or her work. Bonuses don't achieve this. Bonuses are external incentives that at best encourage self-discipline and, moreover, are granted for something the employee would probably have achieved in any case. Praise, however, motivates us for the task ahead because it confirms our own unique abilities. There is virtually nothing that boosts confidence as much as this, so it is important not to take what has been achieved for granted. Instead it should be acknowledged as the fruit of a particular individual's abilities. People are not robots, and a boss who is unable to praise should ask herself whether her work has perhaps lost meaning for her and her task no longer gives her pleasure. What is much more difficult is what St. Benedict calls correction, in other words, rebuke and criticism.

With praise you have to make sure that it is not exaggerated, because it can then sound ironic and almost contemptuous. But it should not be too casual, either, because otherwise it sounds like a rebuke in disguise. Finding the right note for criticism, however, requires immense sensitivity and great self-control, because criticism is always voiced in an already tense atmosphere and for the criticized person much more is at stake than just her professional competence with respect to the matter in hand. In his Rule, Benedict goes into more detail about correction than almost anything else, and what he says proves again to me that knowledge of human nature is not something we have only acquired recently in our modern, psychologically enlightened era.

Let us begin with oversensitive colleagues, the fragile employees whose world falls apart at the slightest disagreement, who are quick to take offense and just as ready to maintain a stubborn silence, and who may even be sitting in the same office. So what can you do when there is a bad atmosphere or when the complaints pile up? I fear only talking can help, taking the initiative and talking openly about the matter. Often you simply do not know what you have done wrong. If I think someone has something on his mind I do not wait until he opens up of his own accord. I speak to him—even and especially when I feel that he resents me for something. While the oversensitive are quick to take offense at others' "rudeness," they are usually equally quick to show remorse about their own thin-skinned behavior, and a patient conversation can not only overcome misunderstandings, but it can also present the opportunity to raise the morale of a dejected person—providing, of course, we have resisted the temptation to behave in such a way as to make the employees afraid of us. One thing we should never do is insist, if our offer to talk is rejected. Let us remain discreet and unobtrusive, even if our motives are entirely philanthropic. We cannot and should not force anyone. But we can and should try to make a person feel less embarrassed if it is shyness that makes him unable to talk.

If an employee has failed in a particular instance, then criticism is due. It should not be necessary to say this, but apparently it is. A female employee of a large concern once said to me, "Where many people go wrong, especially women, is by not criticizing. They are not consistent. They repeatedly ignore the same impertinence and misdemeanors. Very few dare to say anything; hardly anyone insists on a good working climate, and there are many who cannot bear to make themselves unpopular. They buy the sympathy of their subordinates by constantly looking the other way." We will deal with this problem later, but I would just like to say here that I also found it difficult at first to say disagreeable things to people. However, I was soon forced to learn that you do no one a favor by being indiscriminately lenient. Indifference is in any case an affront and always means you aren't taking the other person seriously, either as a human being or as an employee. There are two further aspects to this: no amount of leadership skills will save the person who evades instead of deals with problems. Sooner or later she will be in trouble as problems flare up everywhere, and she will be fully occupied with trying to limit the damage. Nor is it fair to put everyone else at a disadvantage in order not to have to hurt one particular person. This is a question of justice. You cannot have everyone suffering because of a single person. Criticism is therefore in the best interest of every employee as well as of the company, so it would be a serious mistake on the part of a manager to evade this admittedly often onerous duty. Nevertheless, there are still a lot of things to be considered before you criticize, namely, your own motive, the necessity of the criticism, and its effect.

As far as motivation is concerned, your own possibly emotional state is not sufficient reason to criticize a subordinate. You should never do it because you are put out, and never in order to vent your own anger on another person, but always with the basic intention of helping him and furthering the matter in hand. The goal of criticism must be to improve the situation and not to relieve your own feelings. Thus if a boss complains, "I won't put up with that," he must be asked "What do you mean *I*?" It's surely not about him and his peace of mind! It's about the person who made the mistake and the project that is affected, nothing else. Therefore never give way to the desire to criticize simply because you are personally disappointed or already have the person in question in your sights and want to prove that he is useless. Criticism must be factually justified, and there must be no hidden motives.

You must thus always ask yourself whether criticism is necessary or even at all appropriate. I am basically in favor of indulgence, as long as mistakes can be explained by someone having a bad day or by an oversight. Such mishaps should be mentioned once briefly and then, with "it's not the end of the world," forgotten again immediately. A sovereign leader is in any case characterized by composure. He or she is someone nobody should be afraid of, someone who does not make a scene about everything, has a relaxed approach, and bothers others only when something is really at stake. It is not necessary to comment on everything, and the person who goes on about trivial matters simply gets bogged down, loses sight of the big picture, and only causes confusion. Benedict therefore recommends the following with respect to the abbot: "Excitable, anxious, extreme, obstinate, jealous, or oversuspicious he must not be. Such a man is never at rest." How true. The real challenge for every leader in such situations, however, is distinguishing between the trivial and the essential, and here a trait comes into play that is an essential element of sovereignty. Benedict calls it "*discretio*."

Discretio means being able to assess a situation as well as the consequences of one's actions and to identify both relationships and differences; it is thus the intellectual ability to make fine and appropriate distinctions. Benedict mentions it twice in a short section of the 64th chapter, which states: "[The abbot] must show forethought and consideration in his orders, and whether the task he assigns concerns God or the world, he should be discerning and moderate, bearing in mind the discretion of holy Jacob, who said: 'If I drive my flocks too hard, they will all die in a single day.' Therefore, drawing on this and other examples of discretion, the mother of virtues, he must so arrange everything that the strong have something to yearn for and the weak nothing to run from." People in leadership positions do indeed constantly need to make fine distinctions because they are not otherwise able to maintain a sense of proportion, to know whether a dispute is about something substantial or there has been a totally unnecessary counterattack. The former abbot general of the Trappists, the Argentinian Bernardo Olivera, summed it up best with the ironic formula: "Blessed is he who can distinguish one grain of sand from a mountain."

Finally, the question arises as to the most appropriate form of criticism. Here we must, first of all, resist various temptations connected to the natural impulse to want to be right: assuming malice on the part of others, pursuing the question of guilt, and arguing on a psychological or moral basis. None of this is any help in a time of crisis. Where malicious behavior is concerned, when someone makes trouble at meetings or lets us down, it is all too easy to interpret it as a personal attack and a deliberate attempt to test our nerves or expose us. This is a trap we must not fall into! Nothing is gained by suspecting malice, but much is lost—first, because this can easily provoke one into making an enraged remark and thus ruining the atmosphere of the discussion, and second, because you are probably doing the person concerned an injustice. In addition, you lose control of any discussion, because misrepresentations, like everything plucked out of the air, develop their own fatal dynamics. You may by all means consider someone's statements to be idiotic or in error, but you should always interpret the motives of the person concerned as benevolently as possible. The more you maintain your composure, the less you are in danger of wronging someone.

I must also warn against going into the question of guilt when there has been a slip-up. This only makes a complicated situation even more complicated. Any accusation by a leader can be misinterpreted in tricky situations as a moral judgment, with the result that the offender is outraged (and rightly so), because no leader is entitled under any circumstances to make moral judgments. To avoid any misunderstandings, the issue of fault should be shelved, and this makes any mishap much easier to deal with. Of course employees must not be allowed to accuse each other either, whether they are using the incident to take revenge or merely expressing their inability to come to terms with their own failures. I myself have therefore made it a principle not to be interested in who is right. If necessary you can come back to this later to prevent a similar fiasco from happening a second time.

Another point: as a boss you should at all costs avoid explaining the failing of an employee in terms of her character. It is merely another way of making a moral judgment to say, "You were always like this. You apparently haven't learned anything. Now you've done it again." Maybe it's true. But even if a person really does tend to make certain mistakes because of the way she is, this kind of applied psychology doesn't help, because a person's character cannot be changed and such accusations unnecessarily impede resolution of the conflict—quite apart from the fact that it is easier for someone to accept criticism or take a piece of advice to heart if her character is not called into question. A failure should therefore never be used as an opportunity to deal with basic issues unless during a subsequent private debriefing, but every case should be treated as an individual incident. Even after the most massive criticism a person must be able to believe in herself and her value to the company.

However, you will never be able to avoid mortally offending someone or other. Here in Sant' Anselmo, where people from some forty countries work together, I see every day how sensitively people react to criticism. Of course, some people have elephant hides and nothing upsets them. But in general no one wants to hear objections, and if a person has no distance from himself every negative judgment basically calls him into question. Some people collapse immediately because they see even the most objective comment as an attack on their persons, and sometimes the reasons for their reaction are very hard to understand. For example, one of our students from Africa gave the reading in church and forgot to adjust the microphone to his height, so that he could hardly be heard. Afterward I drew his attention to this very gently, with friendly words, but it nevertheless left him distressed. In such moments the history of the last three hundred years of slavery and colonialism resurfaces and suddenly no remark is innocent, no word without connotations, and every critical comment can be interpreted as European arrogance. In a multicultural world, sensitivities of this nature must also be taken into account.

But you must also ask whether you yourself are able to tolerate criticism. Can you take it, for example, if the other person proves to you that you were wrong and your complaints were unjustified? Or are you then distressed and upset? In order for you as the critic not to lose face, there is one rule you absolutely must follow: you must be careful with your choice of words! You must always criticize in such a way that the other person does not feel driven into a corner and still has the opportunity to rectify matters, justify herself, and criticize you. You can, after all, be mistaken, and when you are aware of this you automatically change your style and your approach; you criticize with reservation and behave from the outset with caution and moderation. You should formulate your criticism in such a way that you can back down at any time and concede, "Well, I was wrong." It is also very helpful to ask yourself if you might have made the same mistake in a similar situation. Is this man, this woman really incapable, or has there been an accumulation of minor errors, not all of which he or she could have done anything about? Even efficient people fail, even we ourselves. We should therefore never immediately bring out our big guns; otherwise we may end up simply delivering a furious tirade.

After all that has been said, I should not have to warn against ever giving an offender a proper dressing-down, but I'm still going to do so, because I've seen on any number of occasions how a boss has really jumped on an employee. Here there is obviously an element of sadism. This, of course, goes against all the basic principles of leadership. Everyone deserves respect, even someone who is failing in every way, even the person you have to let go. Of course, there can be the occasional row that clears the air, but only as long as two people are both telling each other a few home truths and it is not one-sided. Usually after a failure you discuss as calmly as possible what exactly went wrong and why, and often the criticized person has known the answer for a long time and is more or less contrite. It is thus absolutely pointless to trample on someone's feelings; it is much more important to restore his badly damaged self-confidence as quickly as possible, while not forgetting that the vehemence of your criticism is always based on your own hurt feelings and never on the severity of the damage caused.

Never let yourself be put off by the first defensive response. As I said before, no one is looking for criticism, and at first the person at whom it is directed still feels too excited and validated by her work to be able to distance herself critically from it. But the first reaction is followed by a second; she continues to process what has been said and with time comes to recognize that the boss wasn't so wrong after all. Much depends here on the reasons given. It is much easier to accept and yield to the inevitable if the reason for a decision is known and understood. In a somewhat different context Benedict also advises that no one should be sent away without being given a reason. If a monk makes an unreasonable demand to the cellarer of the monastery, he writes in the thirty-first chapter of his Rule, "[the cellarer] should not reject him with disdain and cause him distress, but reasonably and humbly deny the improper request." So in any case, the response should never be a brusque "no." The petitioner must understand why her request is being refused. The respect due from one person to another in itself requires that the one who has to cope with a defeat should understand why this is so—quite apart from the fact that you will thus get better results. I remember a confrère once returning the draft of an article to me with the words, "You must write something different. That won't do." I was at first dismayed until he explained, "In reality you are much more confident than your article gives one to suspect. This is not your style." It's true, I thought, after I had read the article again, and I was glad that it had not been published in this form.

Incidentally, there are, as far as I know, four ways of largely eliminating initial resistance. The first is to act like a good coach and simply remark, "You can do better; you've already produced better work." Or you can acknowledge progress and say, "Try again. It's already very much improved, but you are capable of doing even better." Using praise to criticize is in any case the best strategy against basic self-doubt, and here you can even make use of flattery in the vein of "This is exactly the right task for you. You are still, in my opinion, the right man, the right woman for this job. I have every confidence in you."

The second option would be simply to remind the person of what has been overlooked or suppressed. For example, I simply request my coworkers to do this or that and get it off the desk, even though I might feel more inclined to get annoyed with them and ask, "Why on earth is this still lying around?"

The third way is to appeal to the person's professional pride and say, "It's not very good, but the main problem is it's not at all professional." In this way, the criticized person is not likely to take it personally and will do everything possible to prove the contrary. Who wants to be unprofessional?

The fourth method amounts to getting the person concerned to raise the topic of his failure himself. "I send for the offender and begin the conversation in a very friendly tone with personal questions," said a boss who has had very good experience with this method, even in tricky cases. "Then I ask him about his work and through specific questions I get him to reveal his weaknesses himself and talk frankly about his problems. This requires a basic trust. The other person only opens up if he can be certain I won't tear him to pieces." I think that with this final method the real task of a leader, namely being a catalyst, is fully realized. In this way he not only helps the person to obtain essential insights but also makes it easier for him to find the solution to his problem himself.

There is a great deal more to be taken into consideration in this context: the theme of this chapter is inexhaustible because we are talking about the core tasks of the leader, namely, encouraging, motivating, and giving direction, or, as Benedict says, correcting.

I would, however, merely like to touch on two popular mistakes. The first is the temptation to defuse crises by taking control. It happens repeatedly that the department or company management takes over duties and responsibilities after a scandal, on the assumption that similar breakdowns can thus be prevented. This is wrong. First, the leaders put themselves under great strain, and second, they frustrate the employees who are involved because they deny them the opportunity for rehabilitation. That's why I warn against the popular misconception that errors can be avoided by keeping employees on a short leash.

The second error lies in confusing laissez-faire with a humane, sovereign style of leadership. Obviously rebuke and criticism should not cause bad blood, and the person doing the criticizing must ensure that it doesn't leave a bad taste or cause resentment. Ultimately, a boss must in any case be conciliatory. But she must by no means shy away from criticism when it is appropriate. Serious errors must be queried immediately or they will become habitual, either because no one notices what is happening or because everyone thinks it can hardly matter that much. And a person who does not understand or want to understand a gentle hint, who does not respond to an unambiguous warning, must bear the consequences and suffer her misfortune. A boss may not relieve her people of their responsibilities, and a cozy, feel-good atmosphere in the workplace in the end incapacitates the employees just as much as authoritarian paternalism.

Finally, I would like to quote a longer excerpt from Benedict's writings on "correcting," which always fascinate me in two respects: how sharply Benedict distinguishes between the person and his actions and how consistently he links leniency and understanding with unwillingness to compromise with respect to the elementary rules of monastic life. When he sometimes adopts a sharper tone it is also because Benedict's monastery did not just consist of innocent lambs. We must think of the range of conflicting social and cultural backgrounds in his community, which consisted of former slaves as well as patrician sons from the noblest families of Rome, of Italians and Germanic Goths, of trusted monks and suspicious characters, and of priests with their professional pride. When reading the Rule you have the impression now and again that life must sometimes have been quite turbulent in his community. Anyway, this is Benedict's advice to the abbot:

> . . . threatening and coaxing by turns, stern as a taskmaster, devoted and tender as only a father can be. With the undisciplined and restless, he will use firm argument; with the obedient and docile and patient he will appeal for greater virtue; but as for the negligent and disdainful, we charge him to use reproof and rebuke. (Chapter 2)

The abbot must exercise the utmost care and concern for wayward brothers, because it is not the healthy who need a physician, but the sick . . . . Therefore he ought to use every skill of a wise physician. (Chapter 27)

He must hate faults but love the brothers. When he must punish them, he should use prudence and avoid extremes; otherwise, by rubbing too hard to remove the rust, he may break the vessel. He is to distrust his own frailty and remember not to crush the bruised reed. . . . By this we do not mean that he should allow faults to flourish, but rather, as we have said, he should prune them away with prudence and love as he sees best for each individual. Let him strive to be loved rather than feared. (Chapter 64)

CHAPTER 9

A Culture of Two Voices

A Plea for a Female Leadership Style

Sister Enrica Rosanna

Are women leaders different from their male counterparts? Do they behave in conflict situations differently from men? I think women are different from men. They can and should therefore also speak in executive positions with their own distinctive female voice. This is my primary concern. If we women want to be an asset to humanity we must use our differences to advantage everywhere; we must, in other words, strive for a culture that speaks with two voices.

First of all I would like to say that for my work, my way of working, my contact with employees, it was never of any importance whether I was dealing with women or with men. Here in the Vatican, for example, I am surrounded by men, but that does not bother me in the slightest, and it in no way affects my behavior. I do not act any differently with bishops and cardinals than I did in the past with my male and female colleagues at the university or in politics, because for me neither gender nor social position plays a role at my place of work. Here it is the person who matters, nothing else. It may be that some men have occasionally had problems with me, were perhaps initially inclined to underestimate me, but in my experience this soon passes. As long as you behave naturally, do not appear anxious or expect a bonus for being female, men usually acknowledge the authority of a woman.

Nevertheless, women can and should exert their authority differently from men because women have something valuable of their own to offer. This was formerly limited to the private sphere and had no place in society and politics. However, today we as women feel called to use what we have, not just in a particular social area but everywhere in human society. For this reason there must also be differences in the leadership style of men and women. I know that these differences are often barely noticeable in practice, because many women simply copy male behavior patterns on the assumption that they must appear as strong and authoritative as men. Out of fear that they will not otherwise be respected, many neglect to develop their own leadership style. I think this is wrong. After all, our job as women is to move from the biological truth about the two sexes to a culture of two genders, and I would now like to explain in greater detail what I mean by this.

When I say that women ought to develop their own strengths in leadership positions and focus on what they are naturally better at than men, what I am talking about is primarily their talent for looking after the people and things that are entrusted to them. In the history of humankind this concern has been an essential element of female identity. It has always been the role of women to defend the value of life against the values originating from the male culture such as work, power, success, and profit, and I believe the female culture of caring represents an ethical, political, and cultural power source that will make interaction between the sexes much more fruitful in the future—provided it occupies a place in our hierarchy of values that corresponds to its importance.

Female concern can be expressed in many ways, and there are countless examples of this. Mother Teresa has shown us through her care of the poor how to change the world by looking after the ignored and neglected. Monica of Tagaste (331–387), mother of Augustine, the great religious teacher, demonstrated how to bring up children to an awareness of their responsibility. Catherine of Siena (1347–1380) and Brigitta of Sweden (1303–1373) are examples of how to champion peace, namely, in the spirit of loving concern for those who are affected by conflicts and power struggles. Catherine maintained a lively correspondence with religious and political dignitaries and courageously mediated in the dispute between the pope and the secular rulers in Italy. Brigitta, with equal courage, campaigned for a peace treaty during the war between France and England. This concern is the female way of governing, and it was no casual compliment when Mother Teresa was presented at the United Nations as the most powerful woman in the world. This formulation was more an acknowledgment of what power really should do, namely, serve the common good, the community as such.

This concern is a female strength because it is closely related to motherhood, to the fundamental difference between men and women. We only have to think about the nature of the relationship between a mother and the child in her womb, which combines attachment and freedom: attachment because they together form a unit and freedom because at the same time mother and child are two separate individuals. Given this biological fact, it is in my opinion the task of women in leadership positions to connect with people while also creating an atmosphere of freedom, so that everyone can develop his or her identity and discover himself or herself. They should help those with whom they are involved to develop a clear understanding of their own uniqueness, while holding fast to their conviction that all human beings are equal.

Another female strength is the ability to respect limits and understand the purpose of and necessity for restrictions. This is a very important skill, because both in the public and private sphere relationships only last when all parties are willing to accept limits and restrictions. This respect for boundaries is related to the female nature; it is based, namely, on women's experience of not always being fertile, of having periods of fertility alternate with phases of infertility. We women are therefore better able to understand that success is achieved not only by rushing madly ahead but also by stopping and taking time to reflect.

The third female strength is the ability to see pain and pleasure in context. This greatly helps us to bear pain. It is precisely the experience in which the pain of birth is mixed with joy over the newborn child that men do not have. As leaders we can benefit enormously from this deeper understanding of the relationship between pain and pleasure, life and death, conflict and peace, because we have penetrated into the mystery of the seed that falls into the earth and must die before it can bear fruit in abundance. In my opinion women must bring these three unique female abilities to bear in community life and through their own style of leadership; they will succeed in developing a female culture of leadership if they establish connections without binding people to them, if they can recognize and emphasize limits when working with others, and if they cope with difficult situations in the awareness that pleasure can come out of pain. In this way a new executive culture that sees itself as a service to the individual and the community could be created.

Nevertheless, I do not believe that these characteristics enable women to resolve conflicts more easily and better than men. This has not been my experience. What I do see, however, is their ability to be objectively realistic in tense and conflict-laden situations. In this context I like to cite the example of Queen Elizabeth II, who was thoroughly schooled in matters of will and was once told by her governess, "You can achieve anything you want," whereupon the little Elizabeth asked, "Can you get the toothpaste back in the tube?"

Women's attitude to reality is perhaps sometimes less laden with exaggerated ideas of their own importance and greatness than that of men, and this realism can never be a disadvantage in crisis situations. Otherwise I see the principal task of women in terms of preventing antagonisms from developing and fronts from forming rather than slicing through a knot of contradictions. In this age of fragmentation this is highly important; having already lost the center and finding ourselves surrounded by signs of disintegration, we do not need even more fragments.

I also know from many discussions that feminists deny the reality of gender-specific skills and aptitudes and claim that male and female natures are completely identical and cannot be separately defined. This only proves how little they know about what it means to be a man or a woman. I always advise these women to explore this question more thoroughly and give gender differences more serious consideration, and sometimes I succeed in tempering the views of even the most avid of them. I can understand that their bad experiences have led them to see complete equality as a way out. But radicalism is always fruitless. The goal of discussions about gender must be to achieve something that is of benefit and help to everyone and brings everyone together. Total opposition destroys what it alleges to be protecting and preserving.

Radical feminism aside, it seems to me that there is in any case a tendency toward extremes in the relationship between men and women, as if total submission or uncompromising rebellion were the only two alternatives. When I think of my mother. . . . In my family, for example, for my mother everything my father said was sacrosanct. My sister, on the other hand, has the say in her family and my brother-in-law goes along with it. Something similar is evident when you look at the development of feminism. Here there were three phases: uncritical submission to men followed by rejection of everything created by men and culminating in rebellion against men themselves. The foolishness of this radicalism has in the meantime been acknowledged even by the American Betty Friedan, one of the most militant feminists, who revised some of her earlier viewpoints in her later publications.

If you look objectively at the reality of gender issues you must, I find, also reject a number of things that today are no longer solely feminist topics but are widely considered to be right. Among them is a quota of women in the workplace and the protection of women just because they are women. I feel that anyone who is any good should be given opportunities, whether male or female; gender can in no way compensate for incompetence. If a man is more capable than a woman in a particular field, he should fill the post concerned. And one should similarly not be too quick to speak of discrimination when criticism merely happens to offend against the current way of thinking. Discrimination does in fact exist, namely, in the form of economic deprivation and political repression, but criticism does not fall into this category. If unwelcome criticism is avoided on the grounds of discrimination, we lose all our standards of valuation and comparison. There are objective values, reasonable findings, and principles on the basis of which it is not only my right but often even my duty to criticize. Should I refrain from criticism simply because it is not in tune with the spirit of the times?

I give people who go so far as to find contradiction intolerable the same advice I give to feminists. Calm down. Think again about your views and study the problems more thoroughly. And consider accepting the possibility of a model that rejects the equal identity of men and women and helps make the voice of women heard so that in the private sphere and the work environment there can be fruitful interaction between the genders. And be mindful of the fact that focusing on female identity also calls male identity into question—though in my opinion both are requisite for a true culture of two voices.

CHAPTER 10

The Reinsurance Mentality

On Courage and Cowardice in Everyday Business

Abbot Primate Notker Wolf

I have rarely tackled entirely new projects and developed my own strategies, simply because I have no time. One of the few exceptions was the foundation of the first Benedictine monastery in the Philippines, which was really a new departure because we were venturing for the first time outside our traditional mission areas. It meant a lot to me personally and I prevailed in spite of considerable resistance.

Our African monasteries protested particularly vehemently at the time. "We are on our last legs; we need all the people we can get," I was told, "and you are starting something new in the Philippines? Are you in your right mind?" I myself was convinced of what I was doing, but I too was wondering where we were going to get the experienced European monks to set everything up. New foundations always put an additional strain on the mother monastery as well. At the beginning they require intensive support; you must remain in constant contact and fly back and forth, and it is no different from the establishment by a company of a foreign branch. The confrères of the founding community start from scratch in a foreign country, in an alien culture, do not yet speak the language but have to grapple with the authorities; the isolation is an additional burden as well as the anxiety about whether any

local people will join them. Understandably, many people said at
the time that it would never get off the ground. However, we did
succeed, and the Philippines sparked off the foundation of other
new monasteries in India, Togo, Uganda, and the Congo.

To venture into something new requires vision and organiza-
tional skills, but above all courage. Whether in the Order or in a
business, with every step we take into the unknown we revise our
ideas and expect others to do so. We have to take risks, overcome
resistance, and battle against inertia. All businesses, from craft
enterprises to major corporations, are forced to develop at an increasing, and for some people frightening pace, and in this respect
leadership can be described essentially as a culture of courage. It
is not only major ventures that require courage. Managers have to
be prepared for change on any given day: they have to cope with
constantly changing situations, are exposed daily to the unexpected,
and have to make decisions, the consequences of which cannot be
predicted in detail or can be foreseen only too well. A boss is thus
constantly being challenged to show whether she is fearful and
cowardly or courageous.

Leaders should be able to take risks and have the courage to assume responsibility even for difficult and unpopular decisions and
to do what is right. This courage can, however, manifest itself in
many different ways: it need not take the form of willingness to risk;
it can also be reflected in steadfastness, firmness, consistency—in
other words, backbone. In my view courage begins with not letting
yourself be put under moral pressure. For example, people sometimes say to me during negotiations, "But as a man of God, how
can you make such demands? Where is your Christian charity?"
Others who are unhappy about a decision I have made complain
pathetically about my cruelty and the depths into which I am plung-
ing them; they even threaten suicide. I respond to such appeals to
my conscience very unemotionally or, ironically, take the person
sometimes more seriously than he himself does and say, "Well, if
you want to kill yourself, I will not prevent you. I would feel sorry,
but it's up to you." No, we should not be trapped by such attempts
at blackmail. We don't have to take everything personally; there is

only so much we can do, and those who get drawn into everything and relate everything to themselves will become emotional wrecks. The same applies to those who feel under pressure to meet every obligation, to those overanxious people who are permanently afraid of rubbing someone the wrong way and whose consciences will not let them rest until everything is resolved and rectified down to the smallest detail. By being meticulously conscientious you are expecting too much of yourself and others. A boss is neither a benevolent uncle nor a governess and should also be able to let matters of lesser importance rest without being affected by them.

This self-assured composure generates trust. While he can be perfectly willing to admit mistakes, a leader must avoid appearing uncertain or anxious, which is the impression he will give if he justifies or defends himself even before an accusation has been made. Premature self-defense and preventive attacks always draw attention to the weakness of your own position or personality. You should therefore never justify and explain yourself to forestall the accusation of another person. Instead of taking the wind out of his sails, this merely encourages him and fuels his suspicion that you do indeed have something to hide. It is likewise a sign of weakness to present issues in a complicated and circuitous fashion, waxing philosophical about a trivial matter and writing a discursive essay of twenty pages to support an unsophisticated argument. This only indicates that you do not trust your own persuasiveness, as in the situation I mentioned earlier in which expert advice or scientific analysis is cited to justify a decision that common sense would have dictated anyway.

So say what you have to say, briefly and clearly and in English. Of course business jargon, which has infiltrated every aspect of life, has many advantages: it sounds dynamic, and there is nothing managers would rather be. It gives one the aura of someone who possesses the magic formula. It shows you to be a member of an international elite, and no one notices that you are no brighter than anybody else. It also has disadvantages: employees, shareholders, and customers are not quite sure what you mean by "outplacement," "quality gates," or "impression management." And that could also be a good reason why after all it is a good idea to pluck up the courage to speak plain English.

Certainly there are situations in which courage and cowardice are more conspicuous. Painful personnel decisions in particular show whether a boss has backbone, and if it is no longer uncommon to inform people of their dismissal by text message or e-mail, that is clear proof of the inadequacy of management. Cowardly behavior of this nature not only adds humiliation to the misery of the sacked worker but will embitter the remaining employees as well. Such methods are also certain to jeopardize peace within the company, unsettle the employees, and stir up distrust, and are therefore not only reprehensible but foolish.

Dismissals should therefore always be communicated personally. I know how difficult it is for many personnel managers, how many have sleepless nights over it. It always takes courage—unless you are a restructuring specialist and dismiss hundreds of thousands with a cold smile. But you can make things a little easier for yourself and considerably reduce the bitterness of the decision for the person concerned if you communicate a dismissal with the necessary respect for her dignity. My advice is therefore that if a layoff is for economic reasons a personnel manager should make it clear during the discussion that the dismissal is anything but easy for her in order not to offend the dismissed person by implying that she is disposable as an individual. At the same time she should explain as comprehensively as possible why the decision could not be otherwise, so that it is clear that this is not some kind of cruel game but that the current situation has made this step inevitable. In any case a personnel manager must get to the point without beating around the bush, because the person she has summoned has already seen the writing on the wall. Her pain should not be drawn out by leaving her dangling between hope and fear. It is certainly wrong to drive the point home with a sledgehammer, but plain words must be used and it must be made equally plain that the decision was not made for personal reasons.

The dismissed person will still ask why it has to be him. No one can assuage this pain, and in spite of all assertions to the contrary he may well believe that he has fallen out of favor. A wise personnel manager understands that this is a form of self-defense: many people need to delude themselves that they have fallen victim to personal animosities in order to avoid feeling that they are losers. I also find repeatedly that people would rather interpret a dismissal as a personal attack than accept the factual reasons I have explained to them over and over again. As a boss, you have to put up with this; it is only human.

Even though it may not be so difficult to dismiss someone who has not achieved what was expected of her in her job, it still takes courage. It is even harder to remain humane and show not a trace of contempt, and in this situation too one should try to make the decision comprehensible to that person. It might be of help to a personnel manager in this situation to remember that in addition to the internal economic aspect, the issue of fairness to the other employees also has to be considered. The person concerned will always feel unfairly treated, but as a boss you must not forget that all those who suffer under a loser also have a claim to be treated fairly. What does it mean for the group if one person is not pulling her weight? All the others have to work harder or else watch the joint project foundering because of a single individual. This is not compatible with the precept of fairness, and I think sooner or later this will occur even to the person concerned.

It becomes particularly problematic when the managing board wants to get rid of a good man. His colleagues are often faced with the question of whether they should stand up for him and the price they are willing to pay for their solidarity with him. I would ask myself, "Can he be rescued at all? Is my influence strong enough? Or will my protest make me suspect in the eyes of those higher up?" Of course you can argue with the persons responsible; you are entitled to ask, "Is he really so bad? Does he have no merits? Would anyone else be better?" But I fear that colleagues are usually powerless when one of their own falls victim to personnel policy. Then, as hard as it is, you have to accept that some things cannot be prevented. And remember that you are not responsible for the fate of a person when this is in the hands of others. That has nothing to do with cowardice.

The institutionalized form of cowardice undoubtedly has the worst consequences. It is found where there are distinct hierarchies, where class consciousness and snobbery have taken hold and company life is characterized by formalistic hurdles. "This is absolutely awful," a manager affirmed to me. "It demotivates, it paralyzes, and an incredible amount of time is wasted. I know blue-chip companies that have failed because their top managers were too hierarchical, too authoritarian, too bureaucratic. Such people surround themselves with sycophants, and when at some point they go into action they are absolutely certain to make the wrong decisions." I share this view. As a Benedictine abbot primate of an Order that is essentially a rather loose association of autonomous individual monasteries, I already have a strong aversion to centralized and hierarchical structures. But apart from this it can generally be said that those who stubbornly rely on rules and regulations, who emphasize rank and cultivate an authoritarian style of leadership, are well on the way to becoming functionaries. Hierarchical structures are always an expression of irresponsibility and lack of courage, and you can also be sure of finding in these companies a particularly fatal form of cowardice: the reinsurance mentality.

This mentality is rampant and flourishes in every organization governed by the principle that the same mistake must not be made twice—which in practice amounts to a permanent threat. This leads inevitably to a climate of pedantic anxiety, because since mistakes are made constantly everyone now tries to make sure that no one can prove she was responsible for any of them. The result is that every minor detail is noted in a file, every phone call is documented, and the responsibility for every decision is shared by so many people that if worst comes to worst everyone has clean hands. The file proves without exception that everyone did everything properly, no matter how much has actually gone wrong. "I've known managers," the above-mentioned man told me, "who tackle larger projects not with a small, effective troop but with thirty or forty people, so that beforehand everyone has a say and afterwards it's no one's fault if things go wrong. Every meeting is an orgy of self-justification."

In such a climate of fear no proper decisions or humane leadership are possible. Fear is the worst counselor, and anxious people create fear when they take up leadership positions. Why? Because on their way to the top their sense of security is increasingly derived from external structures: precisely those structures that generate fear. Unsure of themselves as they are, they would experience loss of power as the greatest possible catastrophe, which is why they succumb just as easily to the temptation of cowardice as to that of power. An anxious boss can easily be spotted by the employees, no matter how confident she might seem to be, because whenever unpleasant decisions are pending she suddenly has no time. She pays pedantic attention to minor matters and dismisses important issues out of hand. She does not face up to things, is evasive, leaves others out in the cold, and would rather rely on the grudging loyalty of employees who never know exactly how well she is connected with the people at the top than enjoy the trust of free, responsible people.

For a company such leaders are a catastrophe. Bosses cannot take the task of creating an anxiety-free space seriously enough. It's not just a question of the employees' well-being but also of efficiency. It's about the economic success of the entire company. Someone who is anxious cannot of course dispel the fears of others, and unfortunately courage cannot be learned. Nevertheless, it is easier to overcome yourself and your self-doubts if you see your work as a duty and even perhaps consider it your mission in life. So I would like to conclude by telling a brief, quite unspectacular story.

I do not know if she was a courageous woman before she entered the small Italian convent because I first found out about her through her letters. It was in any case an unusual step she had taken, for this monastery consisted only of a few elderly nuns, almost half of them bedridden—it was a dying convent, and on top of this it was located in a large, ugly building complex in the center of the city. At fifty she was by far the youngest there. She wrote to me for advice because she was being victimized by the abbess. Evidently they did not know what to do with her. She unsettled this self-sufficient community, was repeatedly sent away to study, and was sometimes close to despair. We corresponded frequently and I was on the point of advising her to give up when, surprisingly, she was elected abbess. Overnight everything changed. She spoke kindly to everyone, spent the evenings in conversation with her sisters, and within a short time was able to put an end to decades of torpidity, making everyone happy again. "I Christianize interpersonal relationships," she wrote to me. It is quite possible that this convent now has a future again. Where there is happiness, there is life and development. But even if, contrary to expectations, a revival does not take place, she has at least given the old nuns a dignified retirement. I admire the courage of this woman.

CHAPTER 11

A Magic Power

On Listening and Concentrating on the Essentials

Abbot Primate Notker Wolf

During the inauguration of our hospital in North Korea a sister from the Philippines whispered to me, "Father Abbot Primate, please take out your flute and play us something!" We were sitting in a plain and functional hotel dining room, and until then the celebration had been proceeding according to the stiff North Korean protocol. I got up and played something by Mozart on the flute, then changed to Korean folk songs, and lo and behold, everyone's faces relaxed and brightened up and a Korean waitress came and stood next to me and began singing to my flute playing. The assembled company was thrilled. Perhaps our hosts also thought: here we finally have a European who does not have to play first violin but is willing to accompany a Korean woman.

Talking is not everything if you want to give people the feeling you are taking an interest in them and meeting them halfway. Music is of course ideal, because it gives every situation an air of peacefulness and communication, and I even overcame the initial skepticism of my North American sisters in a convivial evening with Broadway melodies. A boss will hardly take out his panpipes to create a relaxed atmosphere, nor does he need to, because a different art has a similarly magical effect on people: patient, attentive, and careful listening. And that has to be learned.

Very few people are really able to listen. Nobody has to be per-suaded to talk. Talking is pleasurable self-realization; it is action and an opportunity to indulge in narcissistic self-portrayal, and so most people feel the urge to talk. Hardly anyone feels the urge to listen; quite the contrary. Increasing background noise makes us more inclined to switch off and inattention becomes a habit that is hard to control. It is at best the media that succeed in getting us to listen for longer periods. Otherwise, listening is for many the dead time between two contributions of one's own to the conversation. It is superfluous, wasted time, and the mere fact that listening re-quires patience and self-control makes it an imposition. We have forgotten the art of listening to such an extent that someone who can actually listen quietly, calmly, and with concentration, even avidly, is regarded as a fabulous or even mythical creature.

However, listening is an ability that has an almost magical power, and no amount of talking is of any consequence if we do not also master this skill. It is not by chance that St. Benedict begins the prologue of his Rule with the word "Listen." The very first sentence reads as follows: "Listen carefully, my son, to the master's instruc-tions, and attend to them with the ear of your heart." He demands the full attention of his audience and expects them to concentrate on the matter in hand with heart and soul. Is this asking too much, given the stress of everyday working life? A godly life or eternal bliss is not, of course, the everyday object of a business concern. But the undesirable developments that can result from inexplicable misunderstandings and the lethargy of frustrated employees who are repeatedly rebuffed by their bosses are reason enough to take listening just as seriously as talking. Listening, thank goodness, is one of the skills you can acquire by practice and will certainly want to acquire as soon as you realize what a powerful effect it has.

Listening does not just mean hearing what is said and picking out the most important information. Of course, you can be glad if communication succeeds to the extent that everybody is able to explain himself or herself clearly. But this is about more than an efficient exchange of information. Listening is the art of prompt-ing your interlocutor through your own silence. Skillful listening has a stimulating effect, encouraging the other person to speak and, even more, to think; it frees the tongue and brain. Listening is often the greatest service you can do for another person, and it requires more from a leader than temporarily keeping silent so that the other person can say something too.

Listening means giving the other person time and space, restraining yourself and bringing her out. For this you must concentrate on her and her alone; you must be able to set aside and forget about everything else and focus entirely on the person sitting opposite you. Your everyday environment must fade into the background and your interlocutor must really have the impression she is alone in the world with you. This cannot be achieved by pretending to listen—women in particular notice immediately when one's thoughts are entirely elsewhere. The attentiveness of the listener must rather be such that she is not already formulating her own answer in her head after the first three sentences, impatiently waiting for a chance to say what she thinks, is not only interested in making a brilliant reply and showing how quick-witted she is, or in getting rid of the other person as soon as possible. She must be like a sponge, soaking up all she hears. She must be absolutely calm, registering and weighing every word, letting the other person say all she has to say and listening to the very end. Only then can she be sure of not having missed anything and only then is it at all useful for her to provide her own input. And only then does the suggestive effect of intense listening have its impact.

What this means is that with my concentration I force the other person to concentrate too, with the result that he speaks more succinctly, all of a sudden finds the right words, explains himself in a more unselfconscious and comprehensible fashion, and sees for himself how certain things relate to one another. The best outcome is that, while he is talking, his problem unexpectedly disappears without the listener having said a word. Listening can inspire the speaker to the point that while talking he suddenly understands everything that until then had been an impenetrable mystery. If someone comes to me who has something on his mind, I let him speak; I listen, and often I don't need to say anything. It usually happens that he says at some point, "Oh, you know, I don't think it's so bad after all," or, "Actually, I should do such and such." "You're right," is my only comment in such conversations, to which I have contributed nothing but my concentrated attention.

Another effect of careful listening is that I learn far more. In this way I discover issues of which the speaker is not at all aware, or I notice that she is avoiding a particular point, that she has not taken something essential into consideration, and that her essential problem lies somewhere else. Just as you can read between the lines, so you can also hear between the words, and then you just have to draw the speaker's attention to what has not been said rather than talk about a solution. You certainly learn infinitely more by intense listening than by listening with half an ear, and you can then ask the right questions. Even if no solution should be currently in sight, the other person may at least be at peace with herself and the world after this talk. She knows that there behind that door is someone who will listen to her, although, or perhaps precisely because, during the entire conversation this person has hardly said anything.

As a boss you are not doing yourself any favor if you let everything go in one ear and out the other or stare ahead of you with a bored expression, maybe play with a ballpoint or leaf through papers and suddenly look up while the other person is talking as if to say "haven't you finished yet?" or indicate in some other way that the conversation is an annoying interruption to your program for the day. I say this because this kind of talk is not just a source of usable information, and as a management tool, listening is just as effective as talking. However, it requires particular effort. Listening has to be learned and repeatedly practiced. It is ascetic in the real sense of the word, as it is a continuous exercise in patience. This in any case is how it is for me.

I really can listen. But over the years I've found it more and more difficult not to interrupt. I have heard so much, and so many things follow the same formula that after the first two sentences I'm on the point of interrupting because I think I know exactly what the other person wants to say, and while he is describing his problem in a rather roundabout way I'm already solving it. If I realize this,

I say to myself, "Wait a minute; whether this is familiar or not is irrelevant. The point is not to produce a quick solution and send him away as fast as possible. With this person you are experiencing a new and unique situation. Let him talk, otherwise you will make the same mistake as you did that time in the school in South America—you are failing to recognize the uniqueness of the situation with all its particular human needs and expectations." A boss must constantly monitor and control himself in this respect. It's not easy to occupy a leading position for many years and still approach every task with the same vigor and openness as when you were a curious, receptive beginner.

Asceticism, patience, restraint, inner distance from things—ultimately it is perhaps the biggest challenge for any manager with her stressful routine to constantly display those virtues that are a recurring subject of this book. The people who are exposed most to the tension between the hectic pace of their work and the need for composure are those who are not shielded by secretaries and assistants, in other words, middle management. They are constantly being confronted with the unexpected, are continuously interrupted and distracted, have to be permanently available and almost infinitely resilient, and are nevertheless supposed to show no signs of fatigue and of course also be willing to take risks even in the knowledge that any mistake could cause a chain reaction. It is an enormous burden. Let us not forget that it is often not the work itself but major errors by management in their dealings with employees that produce stress. You can, for example, be tempted as an executive to do as much as possible yourself, whether out of distrust of the staff or overestimation of yourself. You can load yourself with one task after the other and have no more time for the actual management responsibilities. Or you can let things slide and then suddenly have to help the others if the work is to be ready on time. Should this become a habit, you will be left rushing from one deadline to the next, will no longer know what's going on around you and, because you have already moved on to something else, the employees will wait in vain for feedback. If this escalates, it will no longer be possible to control the department and you will not know which way to turn.

In our monasteries, those at the top are stressed for other reasons, but the end result is the same. Benedict models his ideal picture of an abbot largely on the Roman *paterfamilias*, a family father of the type you can still find in Rome today: conscious of his authority, he is nevertheless perfectly willing to give his children a large say in family decisions. The revival of monasticism in the nineteenth century, on the other hand, was dominated by absolutism masquerading as religion, and today the abbots experience unprecedented resistance because the monks say, "You can't treat us like that; we're adults." In other words, today an abbot has to justify his decisions. He doesn't get very far anymore by insisting on his authority. This can be very wearing over time. It must also be taken into account that the monks always turn to their abbot when there are problems. The abbots therefore easily develop a slightly distorted picture of reality, seeing only problems and hardly noticing how much is actually running smoothly. On top of this they have to shoulder disappointment when monks on whom they have counted leave and when these same monks prove to have deceived them—the confrères are not all saints. The human factor plays a much bigger role in our communities than in the business world. Nevertheless, the solution to all these problems—as in business—is in my view to integrate all those involved and encourage, motivate, and stimulate them repeatedly in order to awaken a feeling of shared responsibility.

I myself, as I have already mentioned, will never finish my work, because I am like that nineteenth-century abbot who confided to his diary: "Today, no time for anything. Constant guests." Never being able to catch up with work is a permanent state of affairs with us too. In my case, however, it has less to do with the guests—although these are numerous at Sant' Anselmo—than with the constant interruptions, the impossibility of being able to work continuously. I've just made up my mind to finish the correspondence when the administrator appears with the terrible news that our building plans are threatened because ancient mosaics have just been uncovered during the excavation work. In Rome this means construction comes to a stop indefinitely. This dashes our hopes for speedy completion of the work. Now I must first console the administrator and then the two of us must look for a way out, and when we are both eventually convinced that the disaster can be averted after all, the correspondence is still waiting for me. In the worst case I pull the emergency brake and say to myself, "That's enough! You're not answering any more phone calls. And no reply is to be longer than four lines!" But if even that doesn't help, then I put all the papers on my desk in a pile, in no particular order but just so that it looks better and enables me finally to go to bed.

As a stressed abbot primate I do, however, have an enormous advantage over secular managers, because in the monastery our time is structured. Four times a day I interrupt my work for Divine Office in our abbey church. Each of these half-hours belongs to God, but it also belongs to me. These are the parts of the day during which I am not under pressure, when I can acquire distance and take a deep breath. Four times a day I stop and experience a wonderful feeling of freedom, however much stress I am under. Another thing makes my work easier: I am not dependent on rapid success. Any sense of achievement is a secondary effect, and I do not acknowledge failures as such because I know that God will grant success in his own time. I need not therefore be discouraged by setbacks.

Managers do not have this freedom, and often they pay a high price for their efforts. For many years they have believed they can cope with their exhausting life through intellect and willpower alone, that their existence is justified by overwork, until they suddenly realize that body and soul are no longer cooperating. They are burnt out. My final advice to leaders in business and politics is therefore to find a balance—not just a temporary distraction, not merely a hobby, but something that is of real importance in their lives. I am thinking in particular of family life that is worthy of the name. And if, despite this, work threatens to devour you, there are still monasteries where you can withdraw for days or weeks and temporarily experience the monastic life—a wonderful way to give yourself time to think and see yourself from a completely different angle.

In a monastery the peaceful environment alone is beneficial. Finding peace is the first step toward being able to think. Once you have reached this point, you should then be supported by an experienced confrère. Self-doubt often appears when everything is quiet around you, and life all at once looks very different. Some people are frightened when they are suddenly confronted with themselves, or after a while they experience wishes and dreams that were previously suppressed by the constraints of their profession. Then it is good to have someone at your side to whom you can talk and who also knows how to gently call you into question. Perhaps you will learn how to do something that few people are still capable of today, namely, to live with yourself. And maybe at the end there will have been a change of perspective, maybe standards will have been revised and long-forgotten things will have taken on a new meaning. You will return to work having acquired true sovereignty and will no longer be afraid of losing power.

I myself sometimes go to the basilica of Santa Sabina, not two hundred yards from Sant' Anselmo. It is one of the ancient churches of Rome that dates from the fifth century. Here there is an old marble sarcophagus with an engraved saying I really like: "Ut moriens viveret, vixit ut moriturus"—In order to live when dying, he lived like a dying man. In more colloquial terms you might say: Remember in time that the world takes everything back. The money goes to your descendants, your title is engraved on your tombstone, your suits are given to Goodwill, and everything else rots away. Of course, older people are more receptive to this point of view than younger ones, but those who have internalized this piece of wisdom no longer cling to external things—and still, they take great pleasure in life.

CHAPTER 12

The Courage to Resist

What Is Expected of Parents and Teachers

Abbot Primate Notker Wolf

I hesitate to move straight from the art of leadership in the field of business and politics to educational issues, because it seems to me that the problems are of another kind, even if, like managers in companies and public authorities, parents and teachers are essentially faced with the task of getting the best out of those who are entrusted to them. But in business and politics there are fairly clear-cut goals to which the resources are ultimately oriented. The need for appropriate management strategies is also indisputable, and their use is obvious. In education today, however, I feel that the goals are unclear, their necessity is generally questioned, and for this reason the resources seem to be arbitrarily chosen. In families and schools there is an uncertainty aggravated by the fact that the benefit of education takes years to make itself felt.

It is therefore worth looking first at the initial situation. A teacher who has been working in schools for thirty years, one of the committed and enthusiastic members of his profession, put it to me this way: "Now we have to pay almost more attention to the parents than the children," he said.

Why? Because nowadays parents either do too much or too little. Either they neglect their children or they overwhelm them and stifle them through their constant concern. In the one case the children are left to their own devices, and in the other they cannot take a single unobserved, unattended step. In many cases parents are completely out of touch with their children. In my talks with parents I thus often have to advise mothers and fathers to establish a reasonable relationship with their children. I explain to them that it is just as wrong to overdo the parenting, to drive their children everywhere and organize everything for them, as to simply leave them to their own devices because of a misunderstood concept of freedom.

He was passionate about what he said but somewhat resigned. He did not doubt the good intentions of the parents, but, like many of his colleagues, he had seen in the last three decades how the pendulum had swung between neglectful and overenthusiastic parenting and had come to the conclusion that the excess in one or the other direction arose out of perplexity. I myself had had similar experiences as archabbot of St. Ottilien. Like many of the old Benedictine monasteries in Bavaria, we also had a school, an academic secondary school, and years ago our principal was already of the opinion that most of the students were over-parented, overprotected and overfunded. "In the morning," he said, "they are taught in school, and in the afternoon parents think they have to make up for the attention they didn't provide in the morning. At the same time, however, they fulfill their children's every wish, spare them everything they might perceive as an unreasonable demand, and have only one reaction to the demands of their offspring: give in, give in, give in." This conversation probably dates back fifteen years or so. At the time I came to the same conclusion, that immoderation was the result of pure confusion.

Amazingly enough, the alarming experiences of teachers, educators, and psychologists are hardly ever reflected in public discussions about education. Where are the new ideas that can give parents appropriate goals, ideals, and principles for bringing up the next generation in a modern, humane way?—the clever, good ideas, or the clever, wrong ideas that issued in the past from the antiauthoritarian experimental laboratory of Summerhill? Where are the ideas that could be talked about, that one could argue passionately for or against? Instead there is silence. Now and then a general feeling of dissatisfaction is aired in a fruitless debate on values, initiated by politicians who after a few rhetorical skirmishes go back to business as usual. Otherwise there has been a spread of fatalism that has all the characteristics of capitulation to the circumstances. The tide cannot be stemmed, it is said, the developments are irreversible, and today you just have to act as you think best and adapt yourself and your standards to the latest tendency. There's nothing to criticize; freedom takes precedence. Give way is the motto, and scarcely has a new need, a new trend emerged than the person who resists it and is reluctant to passively come to terms with the arbitrariness of all values is labeled by those who embrace everything new a stick-in-the-mud.

So should we accept everything? never dare to speak of a crisis? make confusion the rule? I would like to return to my conversation with the teacher mentioned in the beginning. "What we are experiencing," he said,

> amounts to bringing children up to lack independence. In my opinion, what is behind this is pure fear. When I talk to parents I often get the impression that they are afraid that everything could turn out to be a disaster. They meet every suggestion with a frightened "problematic, problematic." And fear is fueled from all sides. Apparently confidence is lacking today. There is neither healthy self-confidence nor what was previously meant by trust in God, the basic assumption that life is well-disposed toward us.

I too know this mistrust of life. It is a strange mixture we are confronted with: on the one hand a paralyzing fatalism that sees every social development as a necessary consequence of freedom, and on the other the suspicion that life could cheat us of all we expect of it. Many of the parents, it seems to me, approach parenting with a basic attitude of resignation and fear, and I would like to look more closely at this tendency.

First, a little story. A confrère at St. Ottilien was looking after a group of bereaved parents, the mothers and fathers of children who had committed suicide or died in an accident. A catastrophe had befallen the parents—especially as it was often an only child—

and my confrère looked after these despairing people for years. He found that many of them were beyond consolation. "The problem is that for most of them there is no life after death any more," he told me. "They no longer see life in this world in a wider context and things only have meaning for them if they are fulfilled in this world. If such people are denied fulfillment in this world, life loses its meaning altogether."

Extreme conditions like these, in my opinion, reveal something that forms a continuous background to the lifestyle of the majority of people: the uneasy feeling that everything is always at stake, all their happiness and the entire meaning of life. Against this background the most negligible circumstances can acquire the greatest significance and the most harmless things can become an existential threat. In other words, we expect the impossible of our earthly life, namely, that it should be everything. And then we blame it for being what it is:—risky, unpredictable, and limited—for cheating us of eternal youth, of the fulfillment of all the excessive demands we make of it, and ultimately of our immortality. Of course, we cannot ultimately come to terms with such a life, and if we are going to trust it at all it has to offer us comprehensive security guarantees. These naturally do not help against the basic problem of life, that it is finite, but they do help us to ignore the fact.

Now an amazing thing happens: our mistrust of life grows to the extent to which we try to insure ourselves against the risks it involves. The safer our world becomes, the more dangerous life seems and the more fear proliferates. Something has gone wrong. Somewhere our reasoning is at fault. This becomes particularly clear to us when we compare our state of mind with that of the people outside Europe or North America. I have often had the opportunity to do so on my journeys to Africa and Latin America and have established that the people there find it much easier to be lighthearted than we do, even though they do not live under the illusion of unlimited opportunities but approach life with realistic and modest expectations, and even though they cannot close their eyes to the fact that life is a risky matter from the first cry of the newborn to the last gasp of the dying. I say to myself that this is precisely why they repeatedly find that life is good to them. They are forced to trust it and are therefore able to develop an attitude of gratitude. And that gratitude, I am convinced, is the crucial prerequisite for a happy life.

This existential realism can, however, only be maintained if we do not look for the meaning of life solely in the life we lead. Whoever expects the fulfillment of all desires in this world is constantly in danger of pursuing a meaningless existence. In this sense our despondent society is the product of a process that has replaced belief, based on hope, in a life after death by belief in this world, a faith based on illusion and repression: we no longer want to accept that life is in all respects limited. And this despondency also suggests to me that today's fatalism is nothing but the wish to at least grab and try out everything that is being offered on the market of sensations. Under these circumstances those who reconcile themselves to the role of indifferent observer are regarded as tolerant, but anyone who dares to take offence is perceived as a spoilsport and silenced with the accusation of being old fashioned.

We seem to have become trapped in a vicious circle: mistrust of life makes us capitulate to the prevailing conditions, and modern fatalism fuels our fear of not getting our money's worth in this life. Parenting has become difficult under these circumstances. Which image of humanity should parents uphold? What goals should they pursue? To which ideals should they orient themselves as parents? A society that makes its own state of development the moral starting point does not help them because its values are fluctuating, indiscriminate, and random; they are dependent on what the media, the entertainment industry, and advertisements present and fill the minds of the public with as reality. They cannot expect much from public debate, because the demand for guidance that is sometimes voiced is not meant seriously. It is an expression of helplessness but not a sign of willingness to move away from aimless individualism. What if the longing for guidance were really to be taken seriously? This would mean first of all recognizing reliable models and goals, and a society that leaves moral principles, values, and ideas of happiness to the discretion of the individual is very far from being able to do this.

Parents today are offered a tempting way out of this dilemma: faith in nature and the innate goodness of human nature. This belief has spread to the degree that confidence in our own culture has disappeared and our cultural values have lost their cogency; supporters of this belief deny the need for education in general, since human beings are by nature good and cannot be improved by their upbringing. And the success of this idea cannot be denied. Nowadays nature is firmly established as the last unassailable constant in our thinking, and anyone who invokes nature in a values debate can be sure of not meeting with any serious resistance. Even the 1968 generation were all for nature, as they declared pleasure to be the guiding principle of human activity and saw in nature the eternal constant that is beyond all suspicion of arbitrariness and manipulation. Since then, everything has been considered good that has as few traces of cultural influence as possible, and many parents want their children to be like their food: ecologically sound and as natural as possible. The best form of upbringing, according to this point of view, is thus no longer to try and influence the formation of will in children or their moral development but to allow their innocent natural dispositions to unfold unchecked.

So nature is the healing force with which to counter a depraved culture? Even this is not really meant seriously. Experience shows that nature is only adequate for the proponents of this belief to the extent that it equips us with instincts. As soon as it gives a hooked nose, small breasts, or crooked teeth, it is bad and has to be corrected. Our relationship to nature is therefore as ambivalent as ever, yet there is a huge difference between traditional and modern perceptions of nature. In the second part of the last century there was a change in thinking about what should be classified as nature and what as culture, about where people could creatively intervene and where they had to exercise maximum restraint. This change is so fundamental that I would like to go into it briefly.

The traditional Western view was that everything that had to do with the human body was fate. That is to say, you had to accept this body as a given, just as it was, with its flaws, weaknesses, and limitations, its subjection to natural fertility cycles and the natural aging process and the constant threat of illness and death. In other words, the body was the product of nature, and nature in the moral sense was neither good nor bad but perfectly meaningful, the expression of a higher reason—which is why the church at all times tried with its norms and laws to protect it from human arrogance. The intellectual-emotional area, however, everything that has to do with character and individuality, was traditionally understood not to be a person's unalterable fate but to be subject to cultural influence. In this area the human being could be shaped, refined, and developed, which was why it was necessary to bend every effort to perfect given abilities and grow emotionally and intellectually. Ultimately this process was also designed to tame the body and subject its instincts to the power of the intellect.

The radical change over the past half century has turned this relationship on its head. It has led to the idea that not the body but character and individuality are fate. All the endeavors of our technically oriented culture today are aimed at the body and overcoming its natural laws, whereas what has become untouchable nature is the intellectual-emotional area. In the final analysis this development renders any form of upbringing futile because nature has neither moral nor cultural standards. It gives parents and teachers no orientation and essentially permits nothing but a resigned laissez-faire attitude. In my opinion, we are on the wrong track entirely when we succumb to faint-heartedness and self-doubt and resort to a belief in the benevolence of nature. This belief has only one, though very questionable, benefit: it gives parents who let their children get away with everything the perfect alibi. If these children later cause problems, the parents are at any rate not to blame. In other words, the belief in nature relieves parents of their educational responsibility with a good conscience.

But in truth, even children are not innocent angels. In the course of their development they have to be brought face to face with a culture that makes considerable demands on their emotional and intellectual abilities and they thus need the help and guidance of self-confident adults. For this reason education is by no means superfluous. But is it still possible in a time of fatalism, of helplessness, fear, and enthusiasm for nature? This is a very real question. I am optimistic and would answer yes, it is still possible, but only as an act of resistance, as conscious, courageous dissociation from common mistakes such as fatalistic indifference. What counts more than ever is thus the personality of the educator. Mothers and fathers—and teachers—must see themselves as real leaders who embody and live out their ideals on their own account without being able to rely on the backing of society, and they must take their function as moral role models seriously, even when such role models in general are exposed to ridicule. This is an enormous challenge, but I can't see any other solution. Values and virtues cannot be achieved through discussion, nor can they be imparted in ethics lessons. They must be experienced by children as a living culture, if nowhere else, then at least in the home and at school.

This is true because children need nothing more urgently than role models and ideals. They are always looking for models, they literally soak them up and learn, grow, and mature by imitating adults. And they are enthusiastic about ideals, as children always have been. My first piece of advice to parents is therefore: rely on your children's enthusiasm. Help your daughters and sons through your own example to acquire a taste for values such as honesty and truthfulness. Youngsters are a bundle of potentialities and eager to experience models in which the best possibilities take concrete shape. Children are struck by the fact that these virtues really can be personified and say to themselves: this is what it could look like if you put your ideals into practice; you could be something like this person. Such experiences are encouraging and inspiring, release energies, and arouse children's curiosity about themselves. They must gradually become aware of their own strengths and abilities and find out time and again that they are not always good enough and fully formed but can transcend their own limits a little every day. How much there is slumbering in young people, how much there is for teachers to awaken and for the children themselves to discover! And all of this is most apt to be brought to life by the example set by the people they encounter.

Let me call to mind just one example of the enormous impact of role models: the late Pope John Paul II. With his straightforwardness and honesty he held up as a role model against the trendsetters in the media who try to dictate to the members of a despondent society how they have to think and act. Such a person attracts attention and is loved, and even if one does not necessarily share his views, such a person can awaken the longing for truth. People like John Paul II are consistent; they don't need to justify their actions; they are immediately convincing. This pope, however, is also engraved on our minds as an exemplary man because he made no secret of his physical decline. His appearances toward the end of his life were almost exhibitionist, but they achieved the desired effect, namely, to make visible again the suffering that has been repressed in public by society. People gladly applauded him when he was bursting with life; now people should also see how things can go downhill with someone. Right to the end he showed that he had come to terms with his approaching death, and this ability to say yes to life, even when it consisted of pain and suffering, convinced many people. From individuals like him we can learn what effect models can have.

But where does one find the courage to be a model, the courage to resist? I understand parents only too well when they despair of their ability to exert influence today. I fully understand that they are tempted to capitulate before the flood of worthless idols produced by the media. I comprehend quite easily that many give up in the face of a society that trims its sails to the wind where moral principles are concerned. Perhaps it might help to make two things clear: first, that parents are not expected to invent their own values and ideals, because our own culture has produced standards of general, almost universally acknowledged validity, and second, that they have no choice but to be models, because the life skills of their children depend on it.

To bring up a child, after all, is to prepare her for freedom. The sole aim of the upbringing process is therefore to help children make responsible use of freedom, and for this their own resistance must be strengthened. This is a task parents cannot avoid, because free decisions are only possible at all when a person has the ability to resist, and only a robust will to resist will keep young people from succumbing to the ever-present temptation to make things as easy as possible for themselves. It would be the biggest mistake of all to expose children to freedom without preparation. The example of parents who themselves have resisted is the most precious thing that can be given to children on their journey to freedom.

Of course, it requires courage to resist the spirit of the times. I would therefore like to remind parents and teachers that they have not been left empty-handed and that the confused helplessness I talked about at the beginning is not an unavoidable fate. It has a cause, and this is the fact that the image of humanity in our culture in recent decades has been robbed of all existential depth, so that a successful life is measured only by external successes. This soulless image of the human person is of course worthless for the purpose of upbringing and education, because external successes are entirely independent of personality. Even a villain can be successful. If we subscribe to this sad apology for an image of the human, we can indeed cease all educational efforts and be content to train children solely with a view to achievement. If there is any purpose to education, it must therefore have in view both the personality of a child and an image of humanity that does not measure the value of a person by external factors.

And this image of the human has long existed. It forms the basis of our own culture. It is the Christian concept that the human being is a creature of God, created in God's image and therefore inviolable and not subject to the control of others. Our claim to freedom and equality is based on this idea, and our human dignity is also derived from it. At the same time, this image takes account of the weakness and gullibility of any individual human. Christian anthropology therefore does not lead to the deification of the human but rather links human likeness to God to human susceptibility to temptation so that we can hold fast to the superior value of humanity without closing our eyes to its imperfections.

In the everyday task of bringing up children this strange ambiguity of human existence must constantly be taken into account. We must assume that children too are exposed to the tension between good and evil without being bad themselves. And we must repeatedly remind them that they can expect both that we will make every effort to support them in their development as human beings who can cope with freedom and that we will have the greatest respect for their individuality and their God-given uniqueness. This is an educational mission that goes far beyond nurturing and protecting or conditioning for success. The Christian view of the human person entitles and commits us to bring up children to be resistant individuals, sufficiently independent to make free decisions. This puts us as parents and teachers back on a solid footing. Our educational efforts have a clear, humane goal. And from this assurance we can also derive the courage we so badly need as parents and teachers.

CHAPTER 13

Believing in Your Own Authority

How We Can Overcome
the Educational Crisis

Sister Enrica Rosanna

I was recently asked during a bishop's visit why fewer and fewer young people feel called to a spiritual life and fewer and fewer want to become priests. I answered, "There are many reasons. But the main one in my opinion is that we are currently experiencing an educational crisis. Because bringing up or educating young people means helping them to achieve personal fulfillment. But many parents do not help their children to acquire a clear idea about life and the world, so that as adolescents they are overwhelmed by the question of what they should do with their lives. Parents are often not prepared for fulfilling their educational responsibility and ensuring personally and as a family that their children develop strong personalities. A decision to embark on a spiritual life however requires a strong personality." That was my answer. Of course, this educational crisis not only affects the vocations. It is after all the expression of an impoverishment that has taken hold of society as a whole and therefore affects all of us. Let us deal first with the greater crises which are behind the education crisis—the crisis of society and the crisis of the family.

When I think of the sociological analyses of the last thirty or forty years, it is our scale of values above all that has changed radically. In the sixties, at least in Italy, faith in God came top in the hierarchy of social values. Today, faith plays hardly any part in the value system of our society. We live in a society which is rejecting Christianity. And this has consequences. It makes all the difference whether I concentrate all my physical and mental energies on enjoying life or whether my life is fulfilled by my faith in God and the enduring values of religion. The greatest danger posed by this development is the loss of practical sympathy for one another that makes us respect the rules of coexistence. We're heading for a society without standards and values, an indifferent society. For such a society everything is in order, everything is permissible, everything is harmless—and the only thing that is frowned on is daring to even perceive ethical distinctions. Pope Benedict XVI summed up the current situation when he talked about a "dictatorship of relativism."

This is certainly also in part the legacy of the late sixties. The parents of today's teenagers are after all a product of the sixties, children of a time when principles were nullified, barriers broken, rules abolished, and spontaneity enthroned. I remember a slogan which was constantly repeated in the years of the youth protests, when I was studying sociology in Trient: "Power to the imagination!" Or, expressed somewhat differently: "All power to improvisation!" This slogan of rebellious teenagers has become a kind of guiding principle for bringing up the next generation. With alarming consequences, since upbringing should never be the result of improvisation—simply because an improvised upbringing opens the door to rampant relativism. Since then, not only the courage to educate has been missing but also the will to do so.

I would like to give an example of the effect this relativism has on upbringing. One of the most important tasks of parents is actually to strengthen their children's willpower. Today, however, fathers and mothers no longer see this as their responsibility. They say, "My child can be as he wants to be." Or, "We let our children do as they like." These children are no longer confronted by their parents with the choice between good and evil, between what is healthy and what is destructive, because their parents themselves barely make these distinctions—and the result is wayward, weak-willed children. However, parents do no better when they do precisely the opposite, constantly plague their children with rules and requirements, spoon-feed them and limit their intellectual freedom until they are either so intimidated that they obey without a word or are so desperate that they rebel. Both a negligent and an over-enthusiastic style of upbringing have the same cause: what's right and proper for young people is at best judged by external standards, with a view to momentary happiness or future chances of success, but no longer by criteria that are crucial for the development of the personality.

And the crisis of society gives rise to the crisis of the family. What has caused this crisis is the fact that the family has lost its internal and external coherence. By external coherence, I mean the identity of the family as a place where we work towards a humane, peaceful society. And the inner coherence arises from the responsibility of the parents to ensure their children grow up to be strong, mature personalities. If the family loses this inner and outer coherence, the only remaining task is to create personal happiness. If the parents' hopes are disappointed, if their wishes are not fulfilled, and if the children do not come up to their expectations, they become depressed and lose all their confidence. The ability to cope with disappointments is becoming increasingly rare, and for this reason fear is spreading, fear of oneself, fear of others, fear of the future, and fear for the children. Precisely because nowadays understanding of the real, important tasks of a family is often missing. But what is also missing is the belief that God is well disposed to people even when not everything in their lives is going according to plan.

So it's a crisis in society and a crisis in the family. Both have resulted in the fact that today many parents cannot identify themselves with their very own educational role. They are simply no longer aware that they are responsible for the formation of their children's identity and for the communication of a reasonable, humane vision of life and the world. They see no relationship between an attitude to life and the world based on true values and the development of their sons and daughters to become strong, responsible individuals who are capable of making free, sound decisions. In other words, they no longer confront the problems of bringing up children. They are not prepared for being parents. For this reason I would now like to discuss the question of what matters when bringing up children. We Salesians are a religious order dedicated to the upbringing and education of young people, so I can contribute much from my experience.

First, bringing up children is an arduous process and has to move forward by small steps if it is to succeed. In ancient Rome, it was considered to be such a difficult business that it was left to the educated slaves. Perhaps we might be more willing to do it if we made it clear to ourselves that bringing up a child is a service of two kinds, namely, a service to the child and a service to the community. Our children and society have a right that we render this service. For this reason we should not be discouraged and should approach our task with the will to do our best.

However, like any other form of leadership the process of upbringing is also an art, which means that all those involved, both children and parents, develop together, learn constantly from one another, support one another, and open one another's eyes. In a family, no one is superior or inferior to anyone else and the youngest member contributes just as much to this learning process as father or mother, so that we should always understand education as an encounter between creative people. It can therefore only succeed if all the parties respect one another's freedom and dignity. Here I am reminded of what a Chinese nun once told me. A Chinese artist, she said, would never complete the background of his picture because he wanted to let the observer use his imagination to fill the remaining empty space. Anyone bringing up a child should proceed in exactly the same way. He should only give him certain ideas or help him to develop certain basic characteristics, while at the same time leaving him free to develop at his own pace, with his own creativity.

Let us beware of constraining and dictating to young people but also of treating them with condescension and arrogance; let us always assume that every child is a new, unique person with individual needs, personal experiences, and specific problems. Let us take the loving approach, the clear-sighted, ideologically unprejudiced approach that allows us to discover the best in our children and understand what is different about them, different from what we might perhaps have expected or might possibly have wished. Let us give them space to develop their gifts and be able to bring their inner beauty as the creation and image of God to maturity, and thus give them the possibility of becoming human beings in the fullest sense. Those who are attuned to young people in this way will themselves benefit from their dealings with them. The Jewish Talmud thus says, "I learned a lot and am grateful to my teachers. I learned even more and am grateful to my comrades, I learned very much more and am grateful to my students."

Children will learn all the more willingly from us the more our educational methods are designed to give them inner freedom and are aimed at conquering their hearts and encouraging them to decide with pleasure what is good and right. We do not, however, achieve this by giving them doctrines and overwhelming them with rules. We achieve it much more by conversing with them on an everyday basis: this ongoing dialogue between parents and children in which all members of the family with their differing characteristics can participate allows parents to offer their children their principles, ideas, and experiences, and enables the children to process the acquired knowledge. More crucial still, however, is the example we give to our children, which they see as an invitation to share in the virtues and values that unite us. Even as adults we repeatedly realize how deeply we are affected by role models. I personally, for example, think of the moving story of sister Leonella Sgorbati, a missionary who had lived a life of passionate devotion to Christ and the poor as a nurse and midwife in Kenya and Somalia and ended this life, the victim of an act of senseless hate, saying, "I forgive, I forgive, I forgive." Such models of faith, hope, and love can make it easier for us to become role models ourselves; but let us not forget that as modern educators we have to take a contemporary image of man as our starting point, have to understand the signs of the times and develop a feeling for the values which are most attractive for young people—peace, justice, and solidarity qualify equally with development aid and equal rights for women or environmental issues.

I will make no secret of the fact, however, that the difficulties of many young people and their passivity stem from the fact that they do not encounter adults of any significance in their lives, starting with their parents and teachers. Many adults are, unfortunately, not role models, have nothing that young people could find attractive, and are faceless and conforming. Because they themselves are not mature, they have no charisma. Above all they are lacking the most important thing that distinguishes an educator, authority, and this seems to me the most worrying finding in connection with the current education crisis. Many parents today no longer believe in their authority, or they even consciously relinquish it in order to be able to interact with their children as friends. In this way, however, they fail as role models, because no child learns from an adult who has no authority; no child in the long run will take instruction from such a person. In other words, to find our way out of the crisis of education, we must have the courage to impose our authority, we must learn once more to believe in our authority. Because authority is a power that serves. It is a power which submits to a task out of love. Which provides orientation without humiliating. Which is willing to be sometimes a teacher and sometimes a student—in the spirit of the Latin "*augere*," from which the word authority is derived—and has the growth and maturity of those it serves in view.

And this authority should be used wisely. In our educational practice we Salesians follow the ideas of our Order's founder, Don Bosco, who gave the young people of his time a simple but also demanding program with the following eloquent formula: "Become an honest citizen by becoming a good Christian." I would recommend three things to parents who want to bring their children up according to this principle. First, that they model themselves on the father in the parable of the prodigal son and set their children an example of forgiveness. Only those who experience forgiveness at a young age can later contribute to the peace of a community and find their own peace. Second, that they practice patience in accordance with the law of life as expressed by Jesus Christ in the parable of the seed that must fall into the earth and die before it brings forth a new, richer life. And third, that they make peaceableness one of their highest educational goals. Peace is certainly a gift of God, but it is also the result of a sincere search, of a highly developed sense of responsibility—which may incidentally be expressed in the most trivial matters of everyday life. It reminds me of the anecdote of the young student who once went to St. Francis de Sales and asked, "What can I do to further peace in the world?" "Don't slam the door so hard," replied the holy man with a smile.

Let us make it clear to ourselves what this means for parents and children: we must all learn to disarm ourselves. We must be ready to completely disarm our hearts. Our hearts are armed as long as we suspiciously and fearfully seek our own advantage and only feel comfortable when we emerge victorious. This attitude does not lead to peace. I therefore propose an ecological commitment that goes far beyond nature and includes oneself as a person. I propose an ecology of the mind, an intellectual integrity that gives us the courage to call things by their proper names and fearlessly name what is bad bad and what is good good so that we become rounded people who can justify their actions and opinions. I propose an ecology of the heart that permits us under no circumstances to side with the powerful and enables us to show love, compassion, forgiveness, and kindness in our own lives. And finally, I propose an ecology of life that enables us to be satisfied with what is necessary, not to be wasteful, and to share everything with joy. Of course this is not an easy route to peace and cannot be pursued alone, because peace is a structure that must be created in dialogue with one another, a fragile structure which is constantly threatened by ignorance, injustice, arrogance, and laziness. For this reason, in addition to constant vigilance, the ability to discriminate is also required, and this is currently not very popular.

I would like to point out in conclusion that all rules and criteria can of course only provide guiding principles for a good upbringing because they must be tailored to the actual person who is entrusted to our care. This is where the family is so important. The family is the place where these rules are not mechanically imposed but applied and modified in the practical context of everyday life and in a very intimate setting, and this alone is what makes it irreplaceable. In addition, a child learns many things from his mother or father alone, not from others—the sense of family, for example, or the feeling of responsibility for a community which repays consideration with love, or the peacemaking value of forgiveness. And what also speaks for the family is the fact that parents believe unconditionally in their child like no one else does. One of the greatest achievements of fathers and mothers is the fact that they never give up on their children even when it becomes difficult to believe unshakeably in them, and they try everything with the confidence that at some point there will be a breakthrough and the youngsters will still show what they have in them. The greatest educational responsibility therefore lies with the parents. However, they have to be able to rely on the cooperation of other institutions, especially the school. Because the school is also a place of upbringing, if it is worthy of its name in the true sense of the word "school," namely a place where young people are freed of the deficits and limitations which prevent them from fully developing their personalities. Families and schools should therefore work together to ensure that every child really develops to the best of his or her ability.

CHAPTER 14

The Existential Dialogue

How We Can Help Children Find Their Identity

Abbot Primate Notker Wolf

"Where did he pick that up?" it used to be asked when, as a child, I used a phrase that was never heard at home. The school playground was one possible explanation or a friend of mine who was two years older and already more a "man of the world." Or perhaps it was advertising on the radio. Those were the only possibilities: outside influences at that time were very restricted. Today they are so extensive that parents are having to accept their loss of monopoly over their children's upbringing at an earlier and earlier stage. Anonymous forces are intervening even in the lives of the very youngest. Who knows, for example, what is going on in children's minds when they watch television? We will never know what seed is being sown in their souls in this way, but the photographer Wolfram Hahn took pictures of the faces of children aged four to six watching television, and the result is frightening. They are sitting slumped and as if paralyzed, with empty eyes and blank faces. They seem fascinated but at the same time dull, absent, and listless, as if their minds, their feelings, in fact the whole little person has been switched off.

For me these pictures indicate a withdrawal from reality. We observe this every day—when a daughter appears for dinner with the family with earbuds in her ears, when a son doesn't move from his computer all day, when teenagers (and adults) abruptly break off a conversation because their mobile phone takes precedence—but this seizure by a higher power is rarely depicted as vividly as in these photos. It seems as if our children slip away into a parallel reality that panders to their fantasies of omnipotence or appeals to their craving for aggression and that they are in any case powerless to resist, while everyday reality is increasingly seen as an annoying or irrelevant alternative world. On top of this is the terrorization by fashion and trends, which starts as soon as children go to school, and the influence of advertising, which convinces even the very young that their personal appearance and image can always be improved. It would not surprise me if fathers and mothers gave up in the face of all this competition. Has education in the real sense become a hopeless task?

I don't think so. I believe that children can still be properly brought up, on one condition: that parents succeed in building up a relationship with their children that is stronger than the external influences. This is not a pipe dream. We have only to remember that a young person is constantly seeking to establish her own identity in all that she does. She will do everything to become the person she is prepared to be in accordance with her abilities, interests, and hopes. For this she needs a community that includes equals but also superiors. She will join the group that gives her recognition as well as the opportunity to prove herself, where she feels she belongs but at the same time can develop a sense of her uniqueness. She will then learn the rules of this group; she will take on its ethos and identify with it. This is the kind of group the family must be. And to establish such a group feeling is, in my opinion, the first and most important task confronting parents today.

I am confident that this can be done, as long as two conditions are met. The first is that parents must be the reference persons for their children at all times, even in the most difficult phases of growing up; they must always be willing to respond to the questions and concerns of their children. German parents seem to find this especially difficult. This was revealed by a UNICEF study in which German teenagers in particular complained that they were not being taken seriously by their parents. More than half of the fifteen-year-olds indicated that their parents hardly took the time to talk to them, putting Germany in last place—after the United States. The other condition is that parents do not curry favor with their children, any more than a leader would do so with other members of the group. Parents should leave no doubt about the rules that apply in the family, and these must be enforced. Parents who keep to clear rules and spend time with their children can be sure of earning respect and by this means also save themselves the endless discussions children get into with their parents when they know that sooner or later the parents will give in anyway. In other words, parents and children should be in constant existential dialogue with one another.

I am reminded of a doctor friend of mine in Rome. His two sons grew up to become splendid young men and his relationship with them is friendly and respectful. When asked how he accomplished this, he replied, "I went traveling with my eldest for two months in Australia after he left high school—just the two of us. During this trip my son discovered what it means to be a father, and I understood better what it means to be a son. My second son is not so keen on adventures, but he is very interested in culture, so I traveled with him for a month through Spain, and on that journey, too, we learned a lot from and about one another."

This man had succeeded in being a credible father, and he had acquired and preserved his credibility because his method of upbringing was not reduced to the banal fulfillment of desires, to bribery by constant accommodation, to compliance with the demands of his children. Instead, he had given his time and attention and had therefore been able to give something infinitely more valuable, namely, orientation, which is precisely what young people need and want most at this age. Joint trips are perfect because they always put life skills to the test. During the journey the attitudes and experiences of the father have to prove themselves daily, and the son increasingly understands the reasons why his father takes this or that attitude. Moreover, the two take each other seriously, and the son also feels acknowledged by his father. It is a very valuable experience. On the one hand the son feels he is of equal value, with the result that the respect he receives from his father becomes self-respect. On the other hand, the son's respect for his father grows as he frequently notices how far his father is ahead of him in experience, knowledge, and life skills. Children become all ears if they think they are going to benefit immediately or can learn something that will be useful to them throughout their lives. This kind of father is certainly an authority who can prevail against the spirit of the times and the media; at any rate, his sons will listen to his advice.

I said earlier that I can only think of childrearing in our time as an act of deliberate resistance. This example should have made it clear why: because bringing up a child means helping her to find her identity, and because in the global consumption and media world there are strong forces trying to prevent precisely this. How many things are aimed at making children dependent and overcoming their inner resistance—advertisements, marketing strategies, pop culture, and of course the always accessible pornography! But humans are creatures who first have to grow in many respects and become stronger and mature in the intellectual and spiritual area. Parents are responsible for ensuring that this development process does not collapse under the onslaught of the media. In my view they therefore have three main tasks: supporting their children in their search for identity, helping them become progressively independent, and laying the basis for a moral pride that will make them free people.

Identity, independence, freedom—I am sure that today these are not automatically seen as the primary goals of childrearing. Much more common is the idea that parents' main job is to make a down payment on their children's future happiness. I think this is a mistake, originated by the sixties generation who declared pleasure to be the highest purpose in life, a principle that has been reiterated millions of times since in advertisements that want us to believe that happiness and satisfaction have simple causes, can be reached by a direct route, and are thus calculable. But happiness cannot simply be fabricated. It is intangible, indeterminable, and as it were a by-product, perhaps as a result of life skills and worldly wisdom and certainly as a consequence of human qualities, but ultimately always a gift. You cannot make happiness the goal of childrearing. You can only create the conditions for it by helping youngsters to approach their lives confidently and courageously. I thus still maintain that independence, cutting the umbilical cord, should be the aim of childrearing. The art of leadership thus consists in this case of the parents leading their children away from them. In other words, like any good coach, parents must work to make themselves expendable and not indispensable.

Children can only be brought up to be self-reliant if they are specifically helped to develop a strong identity, by which I mean the essential core that makes a person unique and also determines his or her self-confidence. How is a strong identity developed? To begin with, identity is nothing more than a mixture of aptitudes and experiences that grows every day of our lives. For this conglomerate to take shape, a child needs people who give him the feeling that he is valuable. That he can rely on himself, because he is strong. A young person must thus primarily receive confirmation from parents who are at all times willing to praise and acknowledge but do not refrain from criticism and reproof where necessary, since the praise of a mother who constantly turns a blind eye at some point becomes worthless. Parents must react to their children: obviously not constantly, certainly not by commenting incessantly, but always when there is something at issue. Both recognition and criticism confirm a child in his identity, and with time he comes to experience this identity not as a random conglomerate but as something special, something unique and valuable. This self-confidence in the long run nurtures his consciousness of his own dignity, and this in turn gives him a certain independence of affirmation from his environment and immunizes him in particular against the bait offered by a consciousness industry that peddles prefabricated identities.

If childrearing is about independence and identity, two methods are automatically excluded, namely, neglect and exaggerated solicitousness—the two extremes mentioned at the beginning of this chapter. Both result in a lack of independence. Parents who more or less leave their children to fend for themselves give them no orientation and undermine their intellectual development, while parents who are over-solicitous, who try to protect their children from every form of shock, frustration, and disappointment, only bind their offspring to them and prevent them from becoming independent. The fact is that children need both freedom and care, and here the art of wise leadership is to find the balance between the freedom parents owe their children and the attention of which the children have equal need.

Why do children need freedom? Because they will otherwise grow up to be dependent, helpless, and anxious people. Children must learn from an early age to deal with problems on their own. And that is why they need to accumulate personal experiences: they have to fall down, find out that the ground is dirty, and get up again; they must test their courage, try the limits of their strength, and discover that curiosity pays off; they must, in short, have confidence in their skills and thus develop a basic confidence in life. Children must thus never be under continuous supervision, handled with kid gloves, and maltreated with over-solicitousness, against which they are defenseless. We do children no favors by wrapping them in cotton wool. I myself have experienced how even as an adult you can blossom when you are exposed to real life. After my first stay in Rome, I was asked by my predecessor at St. Ottilien if I had not been afraid in the chaotic Roman traffic. "No, Father Archabbot," I answered, laughing. "In the Roman traffic I regained the self-confidence that was annihilated in me as a novice."

I would even say that the freedom we owe our children includes the right to let them make their own mistakes. Of course this is hard to bear. It means not protecting them from every danger as well as refraining from intervening again and again in their lives if nothing can be achieved by reasoning with them. But I feel that parents should respect their children's freedom to the point that they can also stand back and watch things going wrong, for example, at school. Young people should not be denied knowledge of the risks of freedom and the experience that one's own behavior always has consequences. Parents must therefore rid themselves of the obsessive desire to prevent with all the means at their disposal what in their view can only end badly. It is also valuable for children to experience the results of their own stupidity or malice. They therefore need parents who can stay on the sidelines, who are able to leave them alone.

I emphasize this because today we are experiencing the exact opposite. Irrational fear has spread among parents, a fear of literally everything: unhealthy food, unsafe toys, and of course unpredictable fellow human beings. Neighbors are transformed into potential kidnappers or rapists, and even teachers have to expect to be accused of abuse simply because they have taken a child in their arms to comfort her. Many parents no longer calculate risks or consider what their child can be trusted or expected to do and what might be too dangerous; they simply assume the worst from the outset and try to eliminate every possible danger. This has a fatal effect on children. Every kind of latitude and freedom of movement is taken away from them, and they are prisoners in their own home, guarded by their own parents around the clock. But the worst thing is that these parents are sending a signal that nothing and no one can be trusted, that the world is full of devils. How, then, should a child actually find the courage to face life?

No, children need freedom. This freedom, however, has nothing to do with neglect. It does not relieve parents of ongoing concern for their offspring. Attention and care are the necessary complement to freedom, because children do not develop to the best of their abilities on their own and of their own accord. They need to be guided in life. Above all, they need people they can trust to guide them, adults who impress them, adults who combine firmness and perseverance with benevolence and strength of character—in other words, adults with authority. A person who has no authority cannot qualify as a model, for in the long run children can't do anything with such adults, whom they at best come to pity and at worst despise, even if it is their own mother. Only authority generates trust, and therefore today leadership qualities are more essential for childrearing than ever. As in the field of management, parents must be assertive and able to motivate and set goals. And like managers in the business world, they must repeatedly say to their children,

"What we are doing right now is worth doing, I believe in it, and that's why we're going to carry it through to the end." This aura of self-confidence and competence is what I primarily mean by the parents' function as models.

One of the most serious errors of the sixties generation was the assumption that authority as such produces fear or is restrictive. It is serious because since then many parents have tried to win the trust of their children in a different way, namely, by indulgence. This cannot work. Parents who curry favor have confused narcissism with love. They are interested in an untroubled, sentimental relationship with their children and want to buy their immediate reciprocal love through constant accommodation. In reality they are thinking less of their children than of themselves. Children, however, usually want nothing to do with this kind of transaction. They work things out in their own way and often use the power they have acquired over their parents to achieve their goals by the easiest route. As a result they develop no powers of resistance, never discover how sweet hard-won victories are, and never learn to deal seriously with reality. Parents who really mean well can thus become uncaring parents who deprive their children of the necessary self-awareness. Genuine love, however, is shown when the parents' aim is to make a child fit for life. This, and not blind indulgence, is the mark of parental love.

Here I think fathers have a particular responsibility. It is usually easier for them than for mothers to be a source of friction, to make demands and put their offspring in their place. Sons in particular experience the natural trial of strength with their fathers as a challenge to their willpower and resistance. I do not mean that fathers should remain in their old roles and be distant from their children. On the contrary, I would like to encourage them to spend as much time with their children as possible. Fathers who play with their children need not worry about their authority; that is automatically respected, because children experience the authority of the father through attention and affection. Nevertheless, even fathers who seek closeness to their children challenge them in a very different way from mothers. It is therefore a mistake to believe that upbringing is solely the task of women, and the children of single mothers have the disadvantage of never experiencing the normal resistance of a father. Children absolutely need both parents; the father plays the role of the person who expects something of them, so that they discover their strength.

I am reminded of the story of a young Lutheran pastor. When he was diagnosed with cancer by the doctors, his bishop did not give him a job that would have allowed him to conserve his energies but instead sent him to the Amazon. The bishop wanted the best for him, and that was not a quiet life at home but the front line, because as a cancer patient he only had a few years to live. Under the harsh conditions of a mission in the Amazon the young man was able to have so many more great experiences that at the end of his life he expressly thanked his bishop for this decision. In reference to childrearing what this means is that the person who truly loves her child will try to set her on a path through life that will enrich her, not in the sense of a vague sort of happiness or material success, but in the sense of being able to cope with life, with all its ups and downs.

CHAPTER 15

Is It Enough to Play the Good Fairy?

What We Owe Our Children

Abbot Primate Notker Wolf

"My three-year-old son is so sweet that I can't refuse him anything," a woman said to me, and smiled so delightedly that I could have no doubt of her sincerity. "I am glad that at least his teachers in preschool can say no. I can't bring myself to do it." She apparently considered educating a child to be mental cruelty, a task for strangers who found it easier to do something so mean. This is what it almost sounded like. In any case she seemed to see education as an imposition, at least as much for her as for her child, because every "no" would be at the expense of the emotional harmony between mother and child and spoil the warm relationship with her son. She was probably one of those mothers who surrenders to the feelings of happiness her child arouses in her and therefore restricts her role to that of good fairy. As a good fairy she need never say "no." As a good fairy she is responsible only for the fulfillment of desires. Such mothers certainly have the happiness of their child in mind when they set him in a little Garden of Eden where he always gets his way. But is it enough not to want to hurt your daughter or son?

Another example: a father, very loving and understanding, conceals his personal point of view on all the important aspects of life from his children. He wants to teach them only objective truths; his own experiences must not count. He therefore leaves them in the dark about his views on politics and religion, and his children, who are now around twenty, still do not know what their father believes. He behaves like this for fear of patronizing them. He wants to avoid all forms of manipulation. He believes he is abusing his authority when he allows his own viewpoint or beliefs to show. His children should encounter life with as few prejudices as possible and preferably construct their worldview on their own, on the basis of their personal experience. But is it really beneficial not to know what your own father thinks?

As different as these two cases are, I find they have something in common. In both of them parental love is combined with the conviction that education is basically equivalent to rape. Both the mother of the three-year-old and the father in the second example believe that a somewhat primitive and therefore healthy identity will emerge in their children of its own accord, and the less influence they have on this process or, to put it more strongly, the less they mess with it, the better. In other words, both of them distrust their own authority and reduce their role as educators to what in their view is a harmless minimum. Maybe they even believe they are fulfilling their maternal and paternal responsibility better than if they brought up their children with a firm hand.

This is not my view, but I do understand their reservations. I know how hard it has become to believe in one's own authority. In the days of the antiauthoritarian rebellion all standards and principles were declared arbitrary, and anyone who continued to rely on norms and rules was suspected of merely acting out his or her desire for power. It had suddenly become immoral to insist on principles, and parents were barely able to distinguish between arbitrary and responsible education measures. Since then, any appeal to principles can be interpreted as a form of suppression, and because few parents want to be accused of that, they would rather forego their authority. The only question is whether children benefit from this.

In this context I often cite an event that happened many years ago. As a deacon I had gone with a youth group to the Tyrol. The participants were fifteen- and sixteen-year-old boys who had never been to the mountains. One day we agreed that next morning we would climb a mountain. The following day, however, the young people decided that this was too much like hard work and protested. I insisted on the excursion. I described the splendid panorama they would see, but still I had to literally drive them to the top. The higher we went, however, the less they complained, and once at the summit their enthusiasm knew no bounds. It had been worthwhile. It had paid off to exact this level of willpower from them. It was worthwhile for these young people because they had now been enriched by an unforgettable experience. And for me, because I had experienced how grateful young people are, in the end, for good, benevolent authority.

This is not so surprising. Only a person who believes in her authority and uses it can release the possibilities in young people. She can enable them to have experiences they would never have of their own accord, can open the door to opportunities and pathways that would otherwise remain closed to them, and can even make it possible for them to experience the triumph of self-discipline. However, she must not make the mistake of confusing authority with authoritarianism. It would be authoritarian to demand blind obedience, but it is quite different to use one's authority to make educational measures plausible, justify attitudes, and insist that a child always keeps to rules and agreements. It would be authoritarian to dictate how a child is to live, but a parent who brings up a child with authority determines the framework within which she can develop. Ideally this framework will be broad enough to give her freedom and narrow enough to provide security and comfort. In my view nothing better can happen to children than parents who use their authority.

Now to return to the mother who sees herself as her children's good fairy: every child has to learn that things cannot always go the way he wants. That is one of the fundamentals of life. Everyone must experience that not all wishes are fulfilled, even if they could be. Delaying fulfillment is an essential element of childrearing. This is how young people learn that renunciation is also an option and is always available as an alternative to fulfillment. Only someone

who has understood this can make free decisions. Otherwise . . . .
We know from past experience what happens. It used to be that it
was the grandmothers who allowed their grandchildren to get away
with everything because they had a purely sentimental relationship
with them. In most cases children brought up by their grandmothers
were unable to cope with life, couldn't bear to be refused anything,
flew into a rage over even minor disagreements, and gave up. People
become independent personalities through friction, not caresses.

I almost have to smirk sometimes when I see how children turn
the tables today. While parents used to have the bad habit of punish-
ing their children by withdrawal of love, it is now the children who
know only too well how to soften up their parents by withdrawing
their love. The good fairies can hardly bear not to be loved, even
temporarily. The problem is that nowadays the parent-child relationship is largely or entirely on an emotional level. It is no longer
the child's future that is the main focus of his upbringing but immediate experiences of happiness and self-love; the result is an
inability to cope with conflicts and tension. Eagerness to anticipate
a child's every wish in order to fulfill it immediately is also detri-
mental to the child's well-being. Here the child is merely the means
to an end, and his wishes are satisfied simply in order to salve the
parents' conscience and rid them of their own responsibility as
quickly and easily as possible. Every form of youthful displeasure
is found intolerable. Even feigned displeasure, even strategically
employed displeasure arouses boundless compassion. You comfort
your child in order to comfort yourself, you keep him in a good
mood to keep yourself in a good mood, you defend him because
you think you have to defend yourself. All thoughts of a child as
an independent person are far removed from such an upbringing.

Alexander, fourteen years old, was the product of this type of
upbringing. He drank, his mother told me, skipped school, stole
money for alcohol, and roamed around at night with his gang.
Once she had to pick him up from the hospital where he had been
taken in a drunken state. She was completely at a loss. She had
thought that letting children have their way was the first command-
ment of parental love. I was not therefore surprised to learn that

her son had no self-confidence at all. How could he, with this kind of upbringing? Self-confidence grows with the difficulties one overcomes, as is evident in sports—for example, in mountain climbing, which is not about top performance but about exertion and the subsequent joy of success. The path of least resistance, however, often leads to alcohol. Of course it will take a lot of effort to put a fourteen-year-old like Alexander back on the right track. He will have to be talked to and told clearly, "This is about you; you are destroying your life." New goals and requirements will have to be made plausible. He will need strict control and patient supervision until he has developed a minimum of self-discipline. And his parents will have to think about a clear strategy, like the coach of a top athlete. But will they ever realize that their previous parenting style was wrong? In no area is it more difficult to admit mistakes. . . .

One father had a completely different kind of experience with his eleven-year-old son after the latter had attended a Catholic boarding school. Though from a good home, the boy had had a reputation at primary school for constantly getting into fights. Since his admission to the boarding school, however, he was a different boy. "Suddenly he stopped fighting," his father told me. "I asked him about this and he told me why straight out. He said, 'There are rules there that apply to everyone and the teachers make sure that everyone sticks to them. That's why I don't need to defend myself any more.' Since then he has never been involved in another fight."

So it's actually quite simple. You only have to understand that freedom is not the absence of rules but is based on rules. You must only have experienced once firsthand as a young person that sensible discipline, a recognizable structure, actually helps you to get your life under control.

With this I would like to return to the father who was so afraid of manipulating his children. I think it is good that he had so much respect for his children's freedom, but in my opinion he failed to recognize that children need a cultural identity, that they have to learn and develop criteria for evaluating the world. While this father gave his children emotional security, he left them stranded intellectually. Nothing, no idea, no worldview, no attitude was to influence them as long as they were still unable to weigh the pros and cons. For fear of influencing them, he kept them away from everything to do with the church, faith, or religion in general: they should decide for or against faith at their own discretion. He thought this too was part of the freedom he owed his children.

I meet such parents with increasing frequency, parents who think they have to restrict themselves to the role of neutral mediator. Many of them, for example, do not have their children baptized so that they can decide freely later on for or against a denomination or the church. The problem is that they have an entirely wrong idea of religion. Religion is not a purely intellectual matter; it is no abstract doctrinal system, the advantages and disadvantages of which you can weigh as if you were deciding to buy something. Religion should not be obvious. It has to prove itself in the course of life, and for this reason a young person must grow into it, must experience a church community, the communal singing and praying, the uplifting of the soul at a moment of profound emotion. In short, she must first acquire a religious identity, and that can only happen if she is exposed to the influence of this religion. This by no means impairs the freedom of a child, because she can still decide against the church later on. But first of all she has to be familiar with what it is she has to make a decision about.

I think: what if the father in our example had been an enthusiastic football fan? If he had then said to his son, "I'm going to the stadium; you stay at home until you are old enough to make up your mind whether or not you like football. When you are eighteen you can decide." This is not very likely since such behavior is totally unrealistic. If children are going to like something, a father or mother must infect them with his or her own enthusiasm, and if the parent makes no secret of his or her passion, a child grows automatically into the parent's world. If the parent does not do this, then others will shape the cultural identity of his or her children. They will be influenced in any case, and there is not much that is a matter of choice: culture is destiny, ordered or chosen as little as one's own skin.

How do such bloodless conceptions of culture come about? In their role as fathers many men evidently shy away from acting as models for their children. Today they no longer have the courage to take responsibility for the children's cultural identity. They prefer to take refuge in the assumption that culture is like a selection of goods from which you take what you want and in the belief that children must know best which of the opinions and convictions on offer are for them. Of course this is wrong. Culture is lived values, which are dependent on mediation by models. But where, I ask myself, can children find role models who want the best for them more than their fathers and mothers? Where can they find role models with whom they can argue so intensively but at the same time trust more than anyone else? Why should parents entrust the cultural education of their children to other people or anonymous forces? At most they seem to hope to be exculpated from blame for their offspring's fate.

No, parents should have the courage to impart to their children what they themselves consider right and important. They are responsible for ensuring that their sons and daughters do not grow up in a vacuum. For this reason I am also of the opinion that the foundation of an established identity can only be laid in the family, not anywhere else, not in a daycare center and not in school, as important as both institutions certainly are. Only children whose essential character is shaped in the family experience their own life history as part of a greater history, and only these children perceive their identity as a variation of a more permanent and comprehensive identity, which in the best case entitles them to be proud and requires them to have self-respect. Being rooted in a family culture with its little daily rituals, its traditions that counter the loss of history in our society, and its structures that make important matters an established part of the daily routine plays a crucial part in the formation of identity. If there are no such roots, children expect no orientation from their parents. I know that the family is often vilified as the source of all evil and the breeding ground of all neuroses. I consider this to be disastrous.

However, it seems to me that the idea that a good world has to be a world of complete harmony is also at work here. This is not a realistic view. Tensions are a sign of dynamism; they need not be radically eliminated but should be endured and made productive.

Nothing would be gained if marriage and the family fell victim to romantic illusions. Promiscuity cannot be an ideal of society. We must remind ourselves that marriage is much more than a legal phenomenon. It fulfills a useful purpose within the culture of a society, because on the one hand with marriage certain obligations are assumed and on the other it is an environment in which primary virtues such as honesty, loyalty, responsibility, and forgiveness are lived and demonstrated daily. These virtues cannot be easily defined and certainly cannot be theoretically taught; they cannot be instilled and controlled like punctuality and cleanliness but must be learned from the example set by parents. We will certainly always have to think about how marriage can be made richer, more loving, and humane. But it cannot be the solution to get rid of it or devalue it by making any form of partnership equivalent to it.

When I plead for a return to the family model I have one thing very particularly in mind: shared mealtimes of children and parents. The meal at the family table is the central ritual in family life. It has a very high symbolic value; it is an expression of community spirit and the essence of the community experience. At lunch or dinner the family takes shape and, even more than family vacations, eating together reinforces the sense of the common bond of all the family members. In addition, at the table children learn to be considerate toward one other. So when parents say, "My child can eat when he wants, there is always something in the fridge," and when I hear that children have to get their breakfast at the kiosk on the way to school, I can see the extent to which the family has disintegrated. I would thus like to point out that children are deprived of fundamental experiences if they are simply allowed to feed themselves. It is not only that these children do not experience their family as a community but also that when meals are nothing but a banal satiation process the consciousness of the sanctity of food is lost as well. And this loss has far-reaching consequences. Self-catering children will hardly develop feelings of gratitude, which are a basic condition for a happy life, as those who are used to simply going to the fridge or to a fast-food emporium when they feel hungry will never have a sense of themselves as recipients of a gift.

All over the world food means more than filling one's stomach. In all the cultures of the world it is an experience in which respect for one another is combined with veneration of the good gifts appearing on the table. We Benedictines too assign the greatest importance to the common meal. We are not only in communion with one another but also with God when we all assemble in the refectory, the dining hall of the monastery, and stand in front of our seats until the thanksgiving prayer fades away. During the meal it is very important to pay the same attention to the food as to the people around you, to pass the bottle of wine or the meat dish, and finally to thank God once more in chorus. The mere sight of the empty dining hall in Sant' Anselmo, with its rows of long tables for more than a hundred people, impresses me whenever I enter it. These long tables always evoke in me the image of the banquet in heaven, which Jesus used as a symbol of eternal bliss. Let us give our children this foretaste of heaven. Let us preserve the custom of the common meal at the family table. Let us not forget that every culture is ultimately based on the experience of community.

CHAPTER 16

Awakening Dormant Interests

Leadership in the Classroom

Abbot Primate Notker Wolf

When I was teaching philosophy at Sant' Anselmo we professors had a relationship with our students similar to that of Aristotle in ancient times with his disciples. In those days we were in close contact with each other, and I often had a whole group of students sitting in my room late at night talking to me about philosophy and God and the world. As a professor you were actually like a spiritual father to your students, and sometimes you could even afford to temper justice with mercy.

I am reminded of a student from Ukraine who was supposed to go to South America to teach, but it did not look as if he was going pass his exams. One day I got his license paper, and on reading it I noticed that each of the three chapters was written in a different style. I went to the library and searched. I found the first chapter in the Jesuit magazine *Civiltà Cattolica*; the second was an article on the French existentialist Gabriel Marcel in the *Revue philosophique de Louvain*. The third author I could not identify and was probably Ukrainian; in any case this part was not original either. The next day I sent for the student and said to him, "Listen, I cannot possibly let this pass. It's plagiarism. But I know you're in difficulties. So this is what we'll do: write it all down again in your own words, so I can see you have understood the material." He did this, and just scraped through the exam.

Decades later I was invited as abbot primate to a festival held by the Basilians, whose house is on the Aventine Hill next to Sant' Anselmo. I went over and was amazed when this same Ukrainian student came up to me. He had in the meantime become the Superior General of the Basilian Order! "If you only knew what a service you did me that time," he said. "You were absolutely right. It was an important lesson for me. And now I'm in charge of my religious confrères from Ukraine to Brazil. . . ."

As I discovered when I was a teacher myself, benevolence plays an enormous role in the relationship between teacher and students—benevolence and the human qualities of the teacher. The art of leadership in the school setting no more consists of cramming students with information, using didactic strategies so they can surmount the next exam hurdle, than leadership in a business consists merely of giving subordinates work to do and getting the maximum out of them. Neither employees nor students work at the push of a button. They are not robots. Employees respond to an inhumane climate in their companies with delaying tactics, by working to rule, or with mental resignation. Students simply do not cooperate or they sabotage lessons if the teacher fails to create a humane atmosphere in the classroom. Both managers and teachers succeed only if they get their people involved in a common project and interest them in a common goal, if they are able to integrate, motivate, and encourage. In other words, both managers and teachers only succeed when their relationship with those who are entrusted to them has a humane basis.

I therefore think the first thing that must be expected of teachers is that they have a fundamentally benevolent attitude toward their students. Teachers must love young people. This is neither sentimental nor romantic wishful thinking, and there are three reasons why it is important. First, as a teacher you work on the off-chance that you will be successful. Apart from verifiable learning success after one or two school years, you will only rarely find out whether your efforts have borne fruit and what this or that student has actually ended up doing. The surprises you can get are illustrated by the example of my Ukrainian student. Everything is possible. For this reason you must never write any student off or brand him a hopeless case. Every student should receive an advance allocation of confidence in his abilities and should keep on receiving this even after repeated failure—not only because you never can say with certainty what is actually in a young person and whether there will be a breakthrough, but also to prevent a child from losing confidence in himself. To fail in this respect is pretty much the worst pedagogical mistake a teacher can make. It may be that a student throws away all his future opportunities himself, but it should not happen that a teacher gives up on a student. As a teacher you must have great persistence, patience, and kindness, and only those who like their students will exhibit these qualities.

Second, children profit enormously from benevolent authority and the feeling that an adult wants the best for them. They will happily cooperate in class when they realize how interested their teacher is in each individual, and they will trust her if she never allows herself to show sympathy for one student or anger with another. School is not only about performance, marks, and professional perspectives but also about the human experiences that can impact one's whole life, and an incorruptible, fair teacher is a model you never forget. One of my teachers was a very difficult person, but when he left the school we were forced to admit that this teacher was always fair. For us he was a model of justice. Students certainly already benefit greatly in their everyday school life from a teacher they can be sure wants to encourage and support them equally. When, however, this is compounded by very personal, human qualities they will benefit all the more. I feel that this benevolence extended to all the students in a class, this respect that takes everyone's desire for attention and recognition seriously, will not be mustered by a teacher who has no affection for young people.

Third, school is not so much about drumming in various facts but about awakening the interest in the world that lies dormant in every child. A teacher should bring his students to a discovery of their own curiosity, which is fundamental to any system of philosophy or scientific discipline. I was a tutor myself when I was a student and later on when I was archabbot, and I particularly liked taking on the "hopeless" cases. My ambition was always to arouse their curiosity about the subject at hand and impart the joy of making an effort, in the belief that every solved problem increases self-esteem. Teaching should be a holistic process; otherwise it is dressage and drilling for mundane purposes. But only teachers who fundamentally like their students will succeed in seeing people in this holistic way.

Such an approach should leave no doubt that the personality of the teacher plays a crucial role in the quality of the lessons. In my opinion personality always distinguishes a good teacher from a functionary of the education system. The problem is that our departments of education see it differently. Ideally they would like to pass a law excluding the influence of personality in the educational sector altogether. Our politicians no longer trust the people, and they certainly don't trust teachers. It is generally accepted that people abuse their authority as soon as they are given some leeway, so it's safer to keep teachers on a short leash by means of grotesquely overloaded curricula and the catechism of the educational theory currently in vogue. It must never be conceded that conventional teaching methods were no worse either! We only have to think of the senseless prohibition of storytelling. There is no quicker means of arousing the interest of the students and holding their attention than by telling stories, quite apart from the fact that the narrative skills of a teacher are instrumental in the development of language abilities in the students. My advice to teachers is therefore that they should take the liberty of structuring lessons with as much variety as possible, combine teacher-centered with student-centered methods and project work with narrative sessions and the use of different media, and show the connection between theory and practice and the relationship between the teaching material and life. In other words, they should not let themselves become slaves of the ruling didactic approach or succumb to the pressure of ideologues who have been trying for decades to eliminate the human factor in education and make teachers knowledge technicians, reducing their role to that of a catalyst. Experience shows that students cooperate when a teacher not only provides knowledge but also has a convincing personality and her own style, is a good storyteller, can also provide background or historical material in science subjects, is authoritative, is fully up to date in numerous areas, and maybe even has a sense of humor and an ironic view of her own self as well.

If some teachers nowadays capitulate before the challenges of the profession the reason is often not so much that that they are unequal to their educational task or inadequate in their subject areas. It is, rather, the fact that the school is paying for both the failings of the parents and the mistakes of the politicians. The former shift their parental responsibilities with increasing frequency onto the school but refuse to support the teacher when there is a conflict, taking the part of their child unconditionally and possibly even engaging a lawyer. These latter misuse schools for their own political purposes and endanger education and educational ideals in the name of social equality. The authority of a teacher in these circumstances is under attack in a very different way from that of a manager in a business. If authority is defined as the ability to maintain an inner balance between distance and engagement, one can imagine the kind of inner ordeal to which teachers are exposed when on the one hand a special pedagogical commitment is expected of them and on the other hand they can only maintain the necessary distance with great effort in the face of the growing number of difficult, undisciplined, and unwilling students. In the face of all that, how can a teacher avoid being worn down by school?

Of course an individual teacher is powerless against political machinations, but his influence in the classroom is all the greater if he sets an example of what he expects from his students. This begins with his appearance. If he thinks he must follow the latest trends of youth culture and dress like his students he is only trying to curry favor with them, and this is immediately interpreted by young people as a lack of self-esteem. They are right.

Blurring the boundary between the sphere of a teacher and that of the students, moreover, is antiauthoritarian hogwash. In addition, a teacher should be a model of courtesy, respect, and self-control. She should not feel she is under attack. She must not let herself be provoked into making personal or ironic comments and must certainly never allow herself to show irritation. However impudent an answer may be, however cheeky a remark, however outrageous an accusation, the teacher should respond with the respectful courtesy that is lacking in the student. A calm, reasonable answer almost always works wonders. The teacher who politely and firmly sets things right, who explains objectively what she requires, will take the wind out of the sails of the biggest troublemaker and create an atmosphere in which conflict can be amicably resolved. The following good example of such an approach was provided by an experienced teacher who exuded a quiet authority.

"My class was in the first period," he said, "and week after week half the students were late. Some regularly wandered in half an hour after class started. I spoke to the class about this. Curiously enough, even those who were notoriously late were in favor of sanctions. One suggested I should create a tally sheet, and anyone who had been late three times would have to bring a cake. I agreed to this, but nothing changed. They delivered their cakes but continued to be late. I brought the subject up once again and now someone suggested simply locking the door of the classroom after class started. Again everyone was in favor, without exception. I then actually did lock the door shortly after eight every day, and—surprise, surprise—everyone was punctual."

I am sure that the escalation of conflict in the classroom can be prevented if teachers have proper conversations with their students right from the start. Of course, teachers are overextended by having to make up for what has been neglected by the parents at home. But they can set an example of civilized manners and create a respectful atmosphere of constructive debate, which should not fail to have an effect in the long run. Still, if nothing works, sanctions must be imposed. It is a simple fact that without the threat of punishment some people see no reason to obey a rule, and individual failure must not be allowed to harm the community as a whole. Teachers should therefore have the authority and legal entitlement to demand obedience and to punish if necessary, regardless of the mood in the class, without having to fear the reaction of parents, and even at the risk of disagreement with the principal, who fears for the reputation of his school every time a child is reprimanded.

Finally, it is the duty of the teacher to demand achievement, for two reasons: first, because children must learn that the fact of working individually or jointly on something is not sufficient by itself and that in the final analysis it is the result that counts. Second, as I said before, because this promotes the self-esteem of the students and gives them the exhilarating experience of constantly becoming wiser and discovering the world through knowledge. Gifted children in particular should be stretched; otherwise they will lose interest in school. As archabbot of St. Ottilien I set my bright young monks to work on the most demanding projects to prevent them from getting bored. Young people who are very quick to pick things up are particularly in danger of subsequent failure if they do not learn soon enough that talent is insufficient without hard work. The education bureaucrats in Europe who are suddenly pushing for performance after the shock of the Pisa study and overwhelming students with subject matter seem to me, however, to be on the wrong track. Spoon-feeding and stuffing the brain with information does not help, and the education crisis cannot be eliminated by robbing young people of the joy of achievement. Effort and leisure go together, because creativity does not thrive under pressure. You must be allowed to gaze at the sky from time to time without feeling guilty.

Teachers usually know this. Meanwhile there are more parents, fathers in particular, who put themselves and their children under pressure to succeed and focus single-mindedly on performance. "No parents' evening goes by," a teacher said to me, "without at least one father waving a brochure and saying reproachfully, 'Here is the latest teaching method. Why aren't you using it?' And he makes it quite clear that he wants to see results a week later." Evidently the misconception that everything can and therefore must be planned has gained ground. Parents want the success of their children's school career, profession, and happiness in life to be guaranteed. For this programs are required, books on the subject have to be studied, and expert opinions must be obtained. Common sense is abandoned; everyone swears by a different method and can hardly wait for the result. "Many parents no longer understand that children develop slowly," said the same teacher. "They expect quick results from every measure, count on prompt success, and if this does not materialize they reject the method employed and immediately turn to the next one. The idea that development takes time is foreign to them."

In this respect we should therefore also make sure we have not allowed ourselves to be carried away by the spirit of the times. Our world is characterized by the belief that everything is technically feasible, that every maturation process can be accelerated and nothing has to be allowed to grow organically any more. That may be true for tomatoes but not for people. Intellectual development takes time. Childrearing and education cannot be approached in the same way as profit maximization in the economy or on the stock market. Otherwise we may end up seeing ourselves no longer as God's creatures, made in the divine image, but only as cogs in the machine, as consumers or as workers, as a commodity of the state and of capital, as guinea pigs for science or raw material for plastic surgeons. No art of leadership, whether in the business world, in childrearing, or at school, is of any use if it is not based on respect for the uniqueness, individuality, and human dignity of those who are entrusted to us and for their freedom and the right to their own life.

A final word: in the second part of our book Sister Rosanna and I have pointed out certain things we consider to be undesirable developments and have spoken about the crisis in society, the family, and education. We would not, however, have taken the trouble to indicate ways out of this crisis if we had thought the situation was hopeless and all efforts to change it for the better were in vain. No, we are optimistic, simply because at our age we have seen that society can also develop in different directions. I think, for example, of our graduation ceremonies in St. Ottilien. In the eighties the students did not take them seriously. They invariably appeared scruffily dressed, and some did not come at all because they considered such celebrations nonsense. The refuseniks just about deigned to visit my office to collect their certificates. Today, however, participation is no longer an issue. Everybody thinks it is important to be present, even wearing a suit and tie. But this is not a resigned return to outmoded forms. The young people do not reflect the rigid protocol of previous generations but behave in an unforced, naturally self-confident manner. Today they are a healthy mix of courtesy and an honest, relaxed demeanor, and it is a pleasure to see them. If Sister Rosanna and I speak of crises, it is in the consciousness that it is always possible to turn them to the good.